D0007748

INCOME DISTRIBUTION

Income Distribution

Fred Campano
Dominick Salvatore

MARY STRIBLING LIBRARY

UNIVERSITY PRESS

2006

OXFORD
UNIVERSITY PRESS

Oxford University Press, Inc., publishes works that further
Oxford University's objective of excellence
in research, scholarship, and education.

Oxford   New York
Auckland   Cape Town   Dar es Salaam   Hong Kong   Karachi
Kuala Lumpur   Madrid   Melbourne   Mexico City   Nairobi
New Delhi   Shanghai   Taipei   Toronto

With offices in
Argentina   Austria   Brazil   Chile   Czech Republic   France   Greece
Guatemala   Hungary   Italy   Japan   Poland   Portugal   Singapore
South Korea   Switzerland   Thailand   Turkey   Ukraine   Vietnam

Copyright © 2006 by Oxford University Press, Inc.

Published by Oxford University Press, Inc.
198 Madison Avenue, New York, New York 10016

www.oup.com

Oxford is a registered trademark of Oxford University Press.

All rights reserved. No part of this publication may be reproduced,
stored in a retrieval system, or transmitted, in any form or by any means,
electronic, mechanical, photocopying, recording, or otherwise,
without the prior permission of Oxford University Press.

Library of Congress Cataloging-in-Publication Data
Campano, Fred.
Income distribution / Fred Campano, Dominick Salvatore.
    p.   cm.
Includes bibliographical references and index.
ISBN-13 978-0-19-530091-8
ISBN 0-19-530091-2
1. Income distribution.   2. Income distribution—Government policy.
I. Salvatore, Dominick.   II. Title.
HB523.C35 2006
339.2'2—dc22   2005020573

While Oxford University Press takes great care to ensure the accuracy and quality of these materials,
all material is provided ''as is'' without any warranty whatsoever, including, but not limited to, the
implied warranties of merchantability or fitness for a particular process.

The product names and services are used throughout this book in editorial fashion only and for the
benefit of their companies. No such use, or the use of any trade name, is intended to convey
endorsement or other affiliation with the book.

9 8 7 6 5 4 3 2 1

Printed in the United States of America
on acid-free paper

HB
523
.C36
2006

To Brigitte and Lucia

Preface

This volume deals with income distribution—a subject acknowledged by economists and other social scientists as being of great importance. Yet there are few courses given on this topic and no book to date that presents a systematic introduction and overview of the subject. The present volume seeks to overcome this shortcoming. By way of preparation, a course in economic principles, a course in statistics, and a course in high school B-C calculus should provide sufficient background to understand the material presented. While the book is intended as an introductory text on income distribution for advanced undergraduate and first-year graduate students, it may also prove useful to professional economists and policy makers. Computer software is supplied to accompany the exercises.

The volume arose out of research conducted by the authors at the United Nations and at universities over the past thirty years. The material in the book has been presented at lectures and seminars at universities, the United Nations, the World Bank, and other conferences in the United States and abroad. Some of the material presented in the book has been published by the authors, singly and jointly, in scholarly journals and volumes on the topic of income distribution.

Contents

1   Introduction   3

2   The Income Concept   14

3   The Income Density Function   24

4   Goodness of Fit   33

5   Alternative Income Density Models   44

6   Income Distribution Summary Measures   58

7   Income Inequality   71

8   Poverty   86

9   Country Comparisons   95

10   Economic Development and Income Distribution   105

11   Growth and Poverty in a Globalizing World   117

12   Redistribution of Income   127

13   Integrating Macroeconomic Models with Income
    Distribution Models   137

    Appendix I: Quintiles Shares and Upper Decile Share of
    Income—Per Capita Income Given in 1990 U.S. Dollars   153

Appendix II: United States: Historical Shares of
Income by Quintile of Household   158

Appendix III: Software Instructions   160

References   165

Name Index   171

Subject Index   173

INCOME DISTRIBUTION

1

Introduction

Income distribution in economics may be either the study of the income returns to factors of production—in which case it is more appropriately referred to as the *functional distribution of income*—or the study of income returns to people or households. The latter is called the *personal or household distribution of income* and is the subject of this book. Income distribution has been a somewhat neglected topic in economics. Although mentioned in most elementary texts on economic principles and given recognition as being an important economic subject, little space is given to its exposition. Furthermore, few undergraduate courses are devoted entirely to income distribution. Income distribution problems, however, are at the core of almost all economic policy.

For example, one of the key issues in the year 2000 U.S. presidential election debate centered around the excess income tax revenue collected. Should it be returned to the people who paid it, which means most of it will go to the higher-income households, which pay most of the income tax, or should it be used to fund a number of government-sponsored social programs, which will mainly benefit the lower-income households? The second alternative implies an income transfer from the higher-income households to the lower-income households. One way to approach this debate is to start with the premise that the decision should benefit as many people as possible, in which case a knowledge of income distribution is indispensable. It is also indispensable to determine which households would qualify for government assistance—for example, to decide what level of household income should be used as a poverty threshold. Likewise, it is useful in deciding progressive income tax rates—that is, what the marginal tax rates should be for the richest 10% of the households, the next richest 10%, and so on. In fact, a knowledge of income distribution would be quite helpful in the debate on whether there should be progressive marginal tax rates at all or, alternatively, a flat tax.

Who benefits if the economy grows by 4%? Would macroeconomic statistics become more meaningful if they are enhanced with income distribution data? For example, if the real per capita income rises from $32,000 a year to $33,000 a year, what difference will it make for the poorest 10% of the population or the richest 10% of the population? How do changes in the consumer price index affect different economic groups, especially the poor? Furthermore, suppose we compare per capita incomes across countries and adjust for the purchasing power of money in different nations, parity, how does poverty in one country compare to poverty in another country?

In this introductory chapter we will indicate the links that income distribution has with micro- and macroeconomics. We will begin with a discussion of wants and scarcity, emphasizing the distribution problem. We will define income distribution in terms of its positive and normative aspects, and we will adjust the circular flow of economic activity to take into account the returns to households. We will also examine labor markets and discuss these.

1.1 Wants and Scarcity

Basic Needs and Human Wants

In the study of income distribution it is useful to distinguish between *basic needs* and other *human wants*. Human wants are satisfied at the discretion of the consumer, once basic needs have been met. Basic needs refer to those goods and services that are vital to sustain life, such as food and drinking water, shelter and sanitation, primary health care, and primary education. All human beings have a right to basic needs. Human wants, on the other hand, consist of goods and services that individuals want but do not necessarily have a right to have. These vary from individual to individual and are subject to changing tastes, technologies, and expectations. We will argue that human wants are insatiable in total, but for most individuals, any one item provides diminishing marginal utility.

Our planet has been endowed with economic resources, which are the inputs or factors that are used to produce the goods and services that humans need and want. They can be classified broadly as land, labor, and capital. For our purposes, land has a more general meaning than just acreage; it includes all natural resources, such as water, air, ores, forests, and fish. Labor will also be generalized to include all human effort, both mental and physical, that can be devoted to production. This broader definition of labor implies that entrepreneurs and management are members of the labor force. Finally, capital refers to the plant and equipment, and it includes inventories, irrigation, transportation, and communication networks that are used in the production process. Note that this definition of capital is distinguished from money that is used to finance the purchase of investment, which adds increments to capital. Note, however, that what is sometimes referred to as human capital is included under our definition of labor.

Scarcity: The Distribution Problem

Resources have alternative uses. For example, municipalities must decide which land will be zoned for residential and which for commercial uses. A computer programmer may spend time programming a video game for children or a war game for the Department of Defense. A field may be used to produce corn for local consumption or coffee beans for export. An automobile plant may be producing family sedans or military vehicles. However, since our planet has a finite amount of any resource, resources are limited and commend a price. Even our atmosphere is limited, and many scientists are concerned that careless use of resources in production will cause a deterioration in the ozone layer, which may end the life-sustaining properties of the earth in the future.

Because resources are generally limited, the quantity of goods and services any society can produce is also limited. Thus, a choice has to be made about the mix of goods and services to produce and which human needs and wants to satisfy. Over time, the size and skills of the labor force rise, new resources are discovered, new uses are found for available land and natural resources, the nation's stock of capital increases, and technology improves. Through these advances, the population may experience a higher standard of living, but human wants always move ahead of society's ability to satisfy them. Thus, the economizing problem can be stated as:

a. Given the limited resources available, what mix of goods and services should be produced to satisfy the basic needs and as much of the wants of the population as possible?
b. What allocation of the scarce resources among producers will minimize waste and ecological jeopardy in producing this mix of goods and services?
c. How can the output be distributed in the fairest way?

This last question is the *distribution problem* and belongs to the study of income distribution. We should also mention here that the distribution of goods and services becomes much more efficient when a society adopts money as the medium of exchange. However, although every sovereign state today has some kind of currency for that purpose, there is still a considerable amount of barter in the world, especially along the borders of developing countries. Even in developed countries, barter arrangements are sometimes made, where goods are traded for services or services are traded for services or goods for goods. One problem for income distribution researchers is to impute the values of such

Table 1.1 Average Earnings by Gender for Full-Time Employees in the United States, 1998

Level of Education	Males		Females	
	Percent of Males	Earnings ($)	Percent of Females	Earnings ($)
Less Than 9th Grade	3.6	23,925	2.2	17,335
9th to 12th Grade (No Degree)	7.5	25,168	5.4	17,218
High School Graduate	32.4	32,647	33.2	23,841
Some College (No Degree)	18.4	39,820	20.7	27,610
Associate Degree	8.1	43,686	9.7	31,959
Bachelor's Degree	19.9	60,605	19.9	39,655
Master's Degree	6.0	72,455	6.8	47,263
Doctorate Degree	1.8	92,255	0.8	65,488
Professional Degree (i.e., M.D., J.D., etc.)	2.2	117,505	1.2	77,103
Mean		44,808		30,671

Source: U.S. Census Bureau, *Money Income in the United States: 1998* (P60–206),Washington, GPO, 1999.

exchanges into the incomes of people or households. Throughout this book, we will only think of income in money terms. In most countries, but especially in the developed market economies, the incomes of individuals will be related to their skills, and the value of an individual's skills are generally related to the highest level of education achieved, as a glance at table 1.1 indicates.

Table 1.1 confirms that both male and female incomes rise with education level. However, education alone does not completely explain income level. Other factors such as family wealth, motivation to make money, and location of residence can make a difference. If it did not, men and women with the same education would have the same incomes. Nevertheless, education is a main factor explaining the income distribution in most countries. Furthermore, those households that have the most income will influence what goods and services will be produced and sold in the marketplace. For example, society produces more goods and services for the average physician than for the average clerk because the former has a much higher income than the latter.

1.2 The Positive and Normative Aspects of Income Distribution

Positive Income Distribution

Much of income distribution is concerned with statistical analysis. More than half of this book will be devoted to statistical techniques that are useful in answering such questions as: What are the per capita incomes of the richest and poorest quintiles of the population? What proportion of the population is below the poverty line? What are the incomes that bracket the deciles (i.e., each 10%) of the households? What is the modal (i.e., the income of the largest group) income? To answer these questions, use will be made of income density functions, which are probability models with characteristics that make them especially well suited to analyze income distribution data. Another statistical aspect of income distribution has to do with the collection of data. Information about household incomes comes from survey and census questionnaires. For example, the Current Population Survey (CPS) conducted by the U.S. Bureau of Census provides household income data as well as demographic data. Most other countries conduct similar household surveys—but not necessarily as regularly as the CPS because of the expense involved.

Normative Income Distribution

There are many unresolved normative issues in income distribution. For example, what should be the criteria for measuring the fairness of the income distribution? What economic system will produce the most ideal income distribution? What income should define the poverty threshold? How should we define basic needs? Should government provide the safety net, or should it be left to churches and other nongovernmental institutions? How much and how should income be redistributed? While this list is not exhaustive, it represents a good sample of the sort of normative issues policy makers, politicians, and economists discuss in connection with income distribution.

1.3 Adjustments to the Circular Flow of Economic Activity

Sources of Income

Figure 1.1 shows the sources of income in all modern societies. Households receive income from government and nongovernmental institutions. By government we mean all levels of government: central, regional, and local. In most countries, government is the single largest employer and is responsible for the wages and salaries of a large portion of the population. Government is also involved in the redistribution of income. It transfers income in the form of educational and financial assistance to the poorer segments of the population from income tax revenues, which are mostly paid by the richer populations of the society. Government is also responsible for the wages and salaries of military personnel (as well as their pensions) and veteran's benefits. It also has pension obligations for retired civil servants and retired politicians. Government pays Social Security and worker's compensation and is often a partner (with the private sector) or the full payer of unemployment compensation.

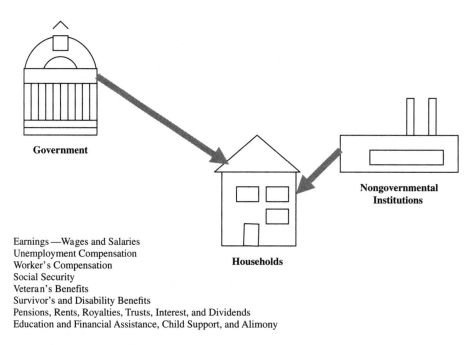

Government

Nongovernmental
Institutions

Earnings —Wages and Salaries
Unemployment Compensation
Worker's Compensation
Social Security
Veteran's Benefits
Survivor's and Disability Benefits
Pensions, Rents, Royalties, Trusts, Interest, and Dividends
Education and Financial Assistance, Child Support, and Alimony

Households

Figure 1.1. Sources of Income

Nongovernmental institutions include all the major producing sectors in the economy, namely, agriculture, industry, and services, as well as churches and other nonprofit organizations. While the government is usually the largest single employer, nongovernmental institutions collectively employ more people. In the developed market economies, the highest and the lowest salaries are paid by employers in this group. For example, some of the highest salaries are earned by the chief executive officers (CEOs) of large transnational companies, while some of the lowest salaries are earned by agricultural workers. Nongovernmental institutions are often also responsible for pensions, survivor's benefits, and disability benefits. Employees in this group may also enjoy dividends from stock in the company given to them as part of their total compensation, as well as profit-sharing bonuses.

Microeconomic Aspects of Income Distribution

Earnings are the lion's share of income. In 1998, the U.S. Census Bureau [4] estimated that the total income earned was $5,467.7 billion, of which $4,403.9 billion was earnings. Thus, about 80.5% of all income comes from earnings. Of the estimated 193.6 million people who have had income in 1998, 146.1 million earned at least part, if not all, of their income.

The importance of earnings as a source of income merits recalling the microeconomic theory of labor markets. The principal finding is that the wage paid and the quantity hired of any particular skill by a firm will be determined by the intersection of the marginal revenue product of labor curve and the marginal cost of labor curve—the former being the labor demand curve and the latter being the labor supply curve. The labor demand curve is derived from product markets; that is, it depends on the demand for the good or service that is being offered. Products that yield high marginal revenue products of labor (i.e., products with high value) reward those with the skills in that labor market with high wages. Hence, a person wishing to maximize his or her earnings potential should prepare himself or herself with the highest paid skill that he or she can master.

Note that this approach to career development does not take into account job satisfaction or the notion that one pursues an occupation that one likes. Table 1.1 shows, however, that there is a correlation between educational attainment and income, the assumption here being that higher education levels lead to higher paid skills. Jan Tinbergen [3] investigated the idea that an extension of the education system may be a means of reducing the gap between the demand for and the supply of the various types of labor used in the production process. His conclusions were that such an approach could improve income distribution; that is, it could reduce the differences in the earnings between members of the labor force.

Macroeconomic Aspects of Income Distribution

One common way to see the linkages between macroeconomics and income distribution is through the effects that changes in macroeconomic parameters such as growth rates, interest rates, government spending, inflation, and population size might have on the changes in income distribution. For this purpose it is useful to specify the income distribution in the shares of income flowing to *quantiles* of population or households. A quantile of population is created by sorting all members of the population by their income from, say, the lowest to the highest. The next step is to divide the population into groups of equal size.

For example, if the population consists of 100,000 households and if they are divided into 5 groups, each group would contain 20,000 households. The highest group, or the fifth quintile, would contain the 20,000 households with the highest incomes. This group would be followed by the fourth quintile, which would be the next richest 20,000 households. The lowest group, or the first quintile, would consist of the poorest 20,000 households of the population. Frequently used quantiles are quintiles, deciles (10 groups), and percentiles (100 groups). Once the groups are created, the share of the total population income flowing to that group is estimated and expressed in percent.

In table 1.2 we see the household quintile distribution of income for the United States in 1998. The first column shows the share of gross income that each quintile has, including government cash transfers but excluding capital gains. The second column shows the income distribution after (1) government cash transfers have been deducted, (2) capital gains have been added, (3) health insurance supplements to wage or salary income have been added, (4) Social Security payroll taxes have been deducted, (5) federal income taxes (excluding the earned income credit [EIC]) have been deducted, (6) state income taxes have been deducted, (7) non-means-tested government cash transfers have been added, (8) value of Medicare transfers have been added, (9) the value of regular-priced school lunches has been added, (10) means-tested government cash transfers have been added, (11) the value of Medicaid has been added, (12) the value of other means-tested government noncash transfer has been added, and (13) net imputed return on equity in own home has been added.

Table 1.2 indicates that income redistribution took place in 1998 through the tax system and government spending since the share of after-tax income of the fifth quintile is less than its share before taxes, and the share of the first quintile is higher. This illustrates how an increase in government consumption might make the income distribution more even if the government channels the spending into programs that affect the poorer populations of the society. In the United States these programs include food stamps, school lunches, housing subsidies, energy assistance, child care, work-related expenses, and medical assistance.

The richer populations of the society can also be affected by the macro-economic policy of the government. For example, any policy that leads to sustained higher interest rates benefits households that derive substantial portions of their income from savings. These people are mostly in the highest quintile. If the high interest rate policy stabilizes prices, then elderly households who are dependent on fixed income streams also benefit, but if the high interest rate policy also leads to unemployment, then households that depend on wages and salaries can be in jeopardy.

High growth or low growth of gross domestic product (GDP) may also lead to changes in income distribution. In both cases, it may lead to a more unequal

Table 1.2 Income Shares of Quintiles of Households before and after Taxes and Government Transfers

	Income Share	
Quintile	Before	After
Highest	49.0%	45.4%
Fourth	23.3	23.0
Third	14.9	16.0
Second	9.2	10.7
Lowest	3.6	4.9

Source: U.S. Census Bureau, *Money Income in the United States: 1998* (P60–206), Washington, GPO, 1999.

income distribution. In the case of high growth, every quintile of population may experience an increase in mean or median income, but the highest quintile may grow faster than the lowest quintile, thereby worsening the income distribution. This happened in the United States between 1993 and 1998 when the income share of the upper quintile went from 48.9 to 49.2%, while the lower quintile remained at 3.6% [4, at xiii]. In 1967 the upper quintile had even a lesser share, 43.8%. Periods of high unemployment and low growth also tend to worsen the income distribution because households in the lowest quintile suffer loss of wages, while the highest quintile may continue to have an income stream from their wealth.

Example 1

Poverty in the Republic of the Philippines

Economists at the National Economic Development Authority in the Philippines estimated that an annual income of 7,400 pesos would be a reasonable poverty threshold for 1992. They arrived at this figure by taking into account the cost of basic needs (subsistence poverty) and adding to that the cost of a consumption basket that they felt characterized those who were living in "continuing low income." The first item in the basket was the cost of a food menu that would provide 2,000 calories per day, as well as the minimum daily requirements of vitamins and minerals. Excluded were items such as alcoholic beverages, cigarettes, and recreation. The nonfood expenditures included the cost of housing, medical care, and education. The gross domestic product for 1992 was 1351.6 billion pesos, with a population of 65.34 million people; thus the income per capita was 1,351.6/.06534, or 20,686 pesos—well above the poverty threshold. However, the World Bank [5] estimated that the upper quintile of population had a share of 48% of the income, whereas the lower quintile only had a share of 7%. That means that the per capita income of the upper quintile was $(.48 \times 1,351.6)/(.06534/5)$, or 48,611 pesos, while the lower quintile had a per capita income of $(.07 \times 1,351.6)/(.06534/5)$, or 7,240 pesos (about \$288 per year). Consequently, about one fifth of the population was living below the poverty threshold.

Example 2

Growth of Per Capita Income in India, 1975–1985

Based on UN estimates, GDP grew from U.S. \$148,592 million in 1975 (constant dollars, base year 1980) to U.S. \$224,970 in 1985. This represents a real growth rate of about 4.2%, but the population also grew at about 2.1%, from 620.701 million people in 1975 to 762.875 in 1985. Hence, over the 10-year period, per capita income went from $239 to $295. While this is certainly an improvement, it did not substantially alleviate the poverty problem for the lower two quintiles. The poverty threshold was set at $280 (constant 1980 U.S. dollars). The World Bank [5] estimate of the share of income flowing to the bottom quintile of the population was 6% in 1975 and 8% in 1985. Therefore, the per capita income of the bottom quintile was $72 in 1975 and $118 in 1985, an improvement but still below the poverty line. Likewise, the World Bank estimate of the income share of the second quintile was 10% in 1975 and 12% in 1985, but the per capita income remained below the poverty threshold at $120 and $177 for 1975 and 1985, respectively.

Problems

1. For the year 2000, country X had a gross income of $90 billion and a population of 3 million people. The estimated income distribution by quintile of population is as follows: the highest quintile has a 45% share of the total income; the fourth quintile, 23%; the third quintile, 16%; the second quintile, 11%; and the lowest quintile, 5%.
   a. Compute the income per capita.
   b. Compute the income flowing to each of the quintiles.
   c. Compute the per capita income of each quintile.
2. Suppose the poverty threshold in country X of problem 1 is $8,000 per capita. What real growth rate of gross income would be necessary to eliminate poverty in 2001?
3. Suppose it is decided that poverty in country X (problem 1) could be eliminated in the year 2000 if the upper two quintiles were taxed the amount needed to raise all quintiles above $8,000 per capita.
   a. Devise a progressive tax scheme that would reduce the shares of the upper two quintiles and increase the shares of the quintiles that need to be brought above the poverty threshold.
   b. Compute the after-tax per capita incomes of the quintiles.
   c. Prepare arguments that justify the amount of the tax share levied against each of the upper two quintiles.
4. Consider the following statement: "If you choose me as your next president, I will improve income distribution in the United States by increasing government spending on education from the surplus of government revenue." To what extent do you agree and/or disagree? Keep in mind the macroeconomic implications of such a policy.

References

1. Intal, P. S. and M. C. S. Bantilan, *Understanding Poverty and Inequality in the Philippines*, Manila, National Economic and Development Authority and United Nations Development Programme, Manila, 1994.

2. Salvatore, D., *Microeconomics: Theory and Applications*, fourth edition, New York, Oxford University Press, 2003.
3. Tinbergen, J., *Income Distribution*, Amsterdam, North-Holland, 1975.
4. U.S. Census Bureau, *Money Income in the United States*, 1998 P60–206, Washington, GPO, 1999.
5. The World Bank, *Social Indicators of Development 1995*, Baltimore, Md., Johns Hopkins University Press, 1995.

2

The Income Concept

In developing countries, especially among the poorer populations, sources of income can be quite different than they are in the developed countries. In many developing country households, wages may not be as significant a part of the total income as income-in-kind. Hence, the definition of income can be quite different from country to country, or even in the same country from period to period. This may not be too important if one is only interested in analyzing the income distribution of a single country for a single year, and the definition of income used is clearly stated so that people reading the results of the analysis understand what is being compared across the income receiving units.

However, if one wants to do a longitudinal study of income distribution, that is, an analysis over a series of years, or if one wants to compare the income distribution across countries, then a consistent definition of income is needed. This is often difficult because the income distribution data that we obtain for most countries comes sporadically from household sample surveys, except in those years when it is obtained from the census. Often, years pass by before a new survey is conducted, and the design of the new survey may be very different than any that preceded it. The budget for the survey is a major factor in its design, and this can affect the definition of income obtained. The United States is an exception in that it has monthly surveys, and income is always included in the March Current Population Survey. However, even in the United States, periodic changes to survey design render them incompatible over different periods.

2.1 Income Definitions

Developed Countries

Before-tax income in developed countries is essentially money income and is usually the *official definition* of income for income distribution purposes. In the U.S. CPS this includes income from wages and salary, self-employment, interest, rents and royalties, Social Security, railroad retirement, supplemental security income, aid to families with dependent children, other cash welfare, unemployment compensation, worker compensation, veteran's payments, private pensions, federal employee pensions, military retirement, and state and local employee pensions. It excludes capital gains, as well as noncash benefits such as food stamps, Medicare, Medicaid, public or subsidized housing, and employment-based fringe benefits. While this definition may not be the most useful for all purposes, it probably offers the most income information for the least cost, since these are items that are easily retrieved from income tax forms.

The estimation of after-tax income is more costly because it requires extracting additional sensitive tax information from the income receiving unit and has the effect of lowering the response rate of the survey. Likewise, the addition of the fungible or imputed value of noncash benefits is difficult because it requires the respondent to keep a tally of the amount of these benefits received. Furthermore, recipients of such benefits may be reluctant to admit that they are receiving them. Hence, the U.S. Census Bureau has developed models to simulate tax data for federal income taxes, state income taxes, property taxes, and payroll taxes (Social Security taxes).

The methodology for imputing the value of noncash benefits, such as food stamps, school lunches, housing subsidies, Medicare, Medicaid, employer contributions to health insurance, and net returns on home equity, is complicated (see Appendix B of Census Bureau, *Measuring the Effect of Benefits and Taxes on Income and Poverty: 1992*, Current Population Reports, Series P60, No. P60–186RD) and also adds to the cost of the income definition. However, these efforts by the U.S. Census Bureau have made it possible for them to provide fifteen different definitions of income (see table 2.1) that may be used for alternative purposes. Definition 2 is the official definition minus government cash transfers. Definition 3 is obtained by adding the imputed amount for capital gains, and definition 4 adds to the definition 3 health insurance supplements to wage or salary income.

Definition 5 begins with the after-tax estimate by subtracting Social Security and payroll taxes, and definition 6 subtracts from definition 5 federal income taxes, excluding the earned income credit (EIC). Definition 7 adds the EIC, and definition 8 deducts state income tax. Non-means-tested government transfers are then added to make definition 9; the addition of the value of Medicare yields definition 10; the value of school lunches is added to get definition 11. Next

Table 2.1 Definitions of Income Used in the United States

Before Taxes
1. Money income excluding capital gains (official measure)
2. Definition 1 less government cash transfers
3. Definition 2 plus capital gains
4. Definition 3 plus health insurance supplements to wage or salary income

After Taxes
5. Definition 4 less Social Security and payroll taxes
6. Definition 5 less federal income taxes (excluding EIC)
7. Definition 6 plus earned income credit (EIC)
8. Definition 7 less state income taxes
9. Definition 8 plus non-means-tested government cash transfers
10. Definition 9 plus the value of Medicare
11. Definition 10 plus the value of regular-priced school lunches
12. Definition 11 plus means-tested government cash transfers
13. Definition 12 plus the value of Medicare
14. Definition 13 plus the value of other means-tested government noncash transfers
15. Definition 14 plus net imputed return on equity in own home

Source: U.S. Census Bureau; *Money Income in the United States: 1998* (P60–206), Washington, GPO, 1999.

means-tested government transfers are added to get definition 12, definition 13 includes the value of Medicare, definition 14 adds the value of other means-tested government noncash transfers, and definition 15 includes the net imputed return on equity in own home.

Once the definition of income is chosen, it is then necessary to decide what the income recipient unit will be. For most countries the household is selected as the basic recipient unit. Hence, income distribution comparisons are made between households. If all households had exactly the same number of people in them, this would be a good choice for a recipient unit. However, they do not. In the United States, estimates of average household size presented in the Census Bureau, Current Population Reports, *Household and Family Characteristics: March 1994*, P20–483, Table A1, show a decline from about 3.33 people per household in 1960 to about 2.67 people per household in 1994. Furthermore, the age of the householder makes a difference. In 1994, for example, householders who were between 35 and 39 years old had the most people in the household (3.32), while elderly householders above 65 years old had on the average less than 2 people per household. Therefore, it is better to do comparisons among types of households with the same basic characteristics—for example, between married-couple families, or between female householder, no husband present, or between nonfamily male householder.

In the United States, income statistics are given for all households, total family households, married-couple families, female householder/no husband present, male householder/no wife present, total nonfamily households, female households (nonfamily), and male households (nonfamily). Clearly, it is important to have as homogeneous an income recipient as possible. If the recipient is "full-time economically active individuals," it is important to keep in mind the differences in income that can be attributed to level of education or to age.

Developing Countries

Generally speaking, developing countries do not have the resources to provide the variety of statistical data found in developed countries. Sample surveys, for example, are conducted sporadically and are often inconsistent with the previous survey done in the same country. Often the sample size is too small to capture a microcosm of the population. Sampling in rural areas can be difficult because they are often inaccessible and do not have facilities such as telephones that might be needed by interviewers.

Because money income may not be the most relevant measure of living standards for the poorest households in developing countries, some surveys try to measure the consumption of households. In this case, the interviewer will try to estimate the household basket of consumption, which could include such food items as the number of eggs, bowls of rice, and pots of tea the household consumes daily. This information is important whether one is estimating the distribution of consumption or the distribution of income. For example, if a household eats 2 eggs a day, and those eggs are obtained from the household's own chickens, then the market value of those eggs can be imputed and added to the money income and consumption of the household.

In one major Brazilian household sample survey done in 1972, interviewers were recruited from the pool of recent graduates of sociology. They were instructed to live with or close to poor households for as long as one month to observe their consumption patterns. One of the surprising results that emerged from this survey was that when poor households purchased food with money, they would buy in small quantities—that is, they would buy 2 eggs rather than a carton of eggs; as a result, they paid more per egg than more affluent households who bought eggs by the carton.

In an effort to standardize household sample surveys for income and expenditure in developing countries, the United Nations issued the *Provisional Guidelines on Statistics of the Distribution of Income, Consumption and Accumulation of Households*. The aim was to improve the collection of survey data from developing countries through standardization. The surveys were designed for a wide variety of uses, including obtaining data:

1. To construct or revise consumer price indices
2. To study the income effect on consumption
3. To study living standards between socioeconomic groups, geographical areas

4. To examine the prices that rich, middle-income, and poor households pay for the same goods and services

Under the guidelines, *total household income* is defined to be the sum of:

1. Primary income
   a. Compensation of employees
      i. Wages and salaries
         a. In money
         b. In kind
      ii. Employee's contributions to Social Security and similar schemes
   b. Income of members from producers' cooperatives
   c. Gross income of unincorporated enterprises
2. Property income received
   a. Imputed rents of owner-occupied dwellings
   b. Interest
   c. Dividends
   d. Rents
3. Current transfers and other benefits received
   a. Social Security benefits
   b. Pensions and life insurance annuity benefits
   c. Other current transfers

Disposable income is approximated by *total available household income*, which is obtained by subtracting:

4. Direct taxes paid
5. Social Security and pension fund contributions

The income and outlay account is completed by computing *gross savings*, which is the result of subtracting from total available household income:

6. Final consumption expenditure of households
   a. In cash
   b. In kind
7. Consumer debt interest paid
8. Other current transfers paid

Mainly because of the marginal cost of adding more information, the UN guidelines are not as comprehensive as surveys found in developed countries. Therefore, the choice of an income definition or income recipient is much more limited in developing countries than in developed countries. Furthermore, even though these guidelines have been in place for almost half a century, the implementation of a systematic periodic household sample survey program is still the exception rather than the rule in developing countries, and researchers interested in examining the income distributions in developing countries consider themselves lucky when they can find any survey at all.

2.2 Income Distribution Summary Tables

Most statistical offices will save the results of a household sample survey in a computer file, sometimes called the *microdata* file. Each record of the file will contain the information of one household. A computer program is then employed to process the file and extract information from the data, which is subsequently presented in the form of tables. One set of tables will be the income distribution tables. These are normally presented in some variation of the format shown in table 2.2.

In table 2.2 the income definition is definition 1 for the United States as seen in table 2.1, and the income recipient is the household. In most tables, only the percentage of households (recipients) or the number of households is given, not both.

Having obtained a table such as table 2.2, the researcher is ready for income distribution analysis. One possible first step in analysis is to show these data graphically. Three elementary graphs that are commonly looked at are histograms, polygons, and cumulative distributions. We can begin to construct these graphs by adding some columns to table 2.2 that give us the height of the histogram, the connecting points of the polygon, and the cumulative distribution.

If we regard the percentage of households that fall into an income level as the probability that a household selected at random from the entire population of households falls into that income level, then the area of the histogram box for that income level will be that percentage. For example, if we select the income level of $20,000 to $24,999 from table 2.2, then the area of the rectangle above

Table 2.2 U.S. Income Distribution All Households, 1999: Money Income Excluding Capital Gains

Income Level ($)	Number of Households	Percentage of Households
Under 5,000	1,357	2.9
5,000–9,999	2,948	6.3
10,000–14,999	3,416	7.3
15,000–19,999	3,323	7.1
20,000–24,999	3,229	6.9
25,000–29,999	3,089	6.6
30,000–34,999	2,855	6.1
35,000–39,999	2,668	5.7
40,000–44,999	2,480	5.3
45,000–49,999	2,200	4.7
50,000–59,999	3,978	8.5
60,000–74,999	4,680	10.0
75,000–99,999	4,820	10.3
100,000+	5,756	12.3

Source: U.S. Census Bureau, *Money Income in the United States: 1999* (P60–209), Washington, GPO, 2000.

Table 2.3 U.S. Income Distribution All Households, 1999:
Money Income Excluding Capital Gains

Income Level ($)	Width	% of HH	Height	Cum %
Under 5,000	5,000	2.9	.00058	2.9
5,000–9,999	5,000	6.3	.00126	9.2
10,000–14,999	5,000	7.3	.00146	16.5
15,000–19,999	5,000	7.1	.00142	23.6
20,000–24,999	5,000	6.9	.00138	30.5
25,000–29,999	5,000	6.6	.00132	37.1
30,000–34,999	5,000	6.1	.00122	43.2
35,000–39,999	5,000	5.7	.00114	48.9
40,000–44,999	5,000	5.3	.00106	54.2
45,000–49,999	5,000	4.7	.00094	58.9
50,000–59,999	10,000	8.5	.00085	67.4
60,000–74,999	15,000	10.0	.00067	77.4
75,000–99,999	25,000	10.3	.000412	87.7
100,000+	—	12.3		100

the income level will be 6.9%. To get the height of that rectangle, we must divide the width of the rectangle ($5,000 = $24,999 − $20,000 + $1) into the area 6.9%. The result is 6.9/5,000 = 0.00138. Table 2.3 shows the computations for the entire distribution.

Notice that the last income level (above $100,000) is not closed; therefore, it cannot be represented in a rectangle and hence must be excluded from the histogram. Using the graphics software in a spreadsheet program, the histogram for the data in table 2.3 is shown in figure 2.1. The histogram reveals the shape of the income distribution. In this case, the mode of the distribution is

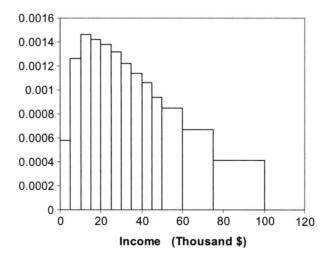

Figure 2.1. Histogram

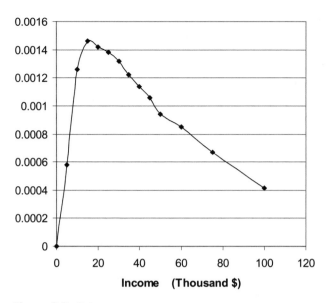

Figure 2.2. Polygon

far to the left and seems to lie between $10,000 and $15,000, in the third income level.

The corresponding polygon is shown in figure 2.2. The polygon is the concave envelope around the histogram, and it too indicates a right-sided skewness to the distribution.

Figure 2.3 shows the cumulative distribution function. From this diagram, one can see the percentage of households that have income below any level.

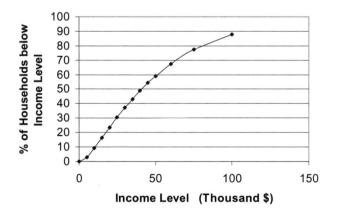

Figure 2.3. Cumulative Distribution

2.3 Comparing Income Distributions

Temporal Comparisons

Often researchers are interested in how the income distribution of a country, or of a group within a country, has changed from one period to another. Such comparisons are valid when the sample survey design is consistent over the two periods. This of course implies that the income definition has not changed and that the sample is capturing the same microcosm of the population in both periods. This is difficult to do when the periods are spread over long periods of time, say, 10 years or more.

Demographic shifts in the population, changes in income sources and consumption patterns, and changes in the goals of the survey can all can lead to inconsistent designs. Survey design can also be affected by changes in the personnel who conduct the survey or by a change in the agency responsible for the survey. Hence, it is the responsibility of the researcher to check the surveys before any conclusions are drawn from comparisons. Sometimes adjustments can be made that will compensate for any inconsistencies. It is better, however, to consult with statisticians of the responsible agency before making any adjustments.

Cross-Country Comparisons

Comparing income distributions between countries is more difficult than temporal comparisons for a given country because the researcher is faced with all of the same problems of temporal comparisons, plus a whole host of others associated with the socioeconomic differences between countries. It is for these reasons that the United Nations established the guidelines mentioned earlier. However, in those cases where there is enough in common in the surveys between two (or more) countries (so that the researcher feels a reasonably fair comparison can be made) the comparison would probably benefit if the income units were adjusted to purchasing power parity exchange rates. The authoritative source for these is the latest issue of *World Product and Income: International Comparisons of Real Gross Product*, a joint United Nations/World Bank publication. This is based on pioneering work by Irving Kravis, Alan Heston, and Robert Summers of the University of Pennsylvania.

Problems

1. Obtain the U.S. Census publication *Money Income in the United States: 1999* (P60–209) from a library that collects government documents or, alternatively, download it using the following steps:

a. The URL is http://www.census.gov.
b. Select people and then income.
c. Follow instructions for downloading the publication.

2. Find the summary table for the income distribution for all households under definition 15 in *Money Income in the United States: 1999* (P60–209) (table 13).

a. Construct a histogram for the above distribution and graph it using graphic software, for example, the graph wizard in *Microsoft EXCEL.*

Hint: You will have to select the "scatter type" graph option and specify the coordinates of the corners of every rectangle, as in the example below:

Income	Height
0	0.00058
5	0.00058
5	0
5	0.00126
10	0.00126
10	0
10	0.00146
15	0.00146
15	0
15	0.00142
20	0.00142
20	0
20	0.00138

The above coordinates will allow you to draw the four rectangles over the income levels 0–$4,999, $5,000–$9,999, $10,000–$14,999, and $15,000–$19,999 in figure 2.1. To complete the histogram the coordinates for the remaining rectangles must be specified.

b. Graph the polygon for the distribution. In this case it is only necessary to specify the coordinates as they are shown in table 2.3 with the addition of (0, 0). Hence the pairs are (0, 0), (5, .00058), (10, .00126), (15, .00146), and so on. *Note*: You will have different heights than these.
c. Graph the cumulative distribution function for the distribution. The coordinates are also taken from table 2.3, namely, (0, 0), (5, 2.9), (10, 9.2), and so on.

Reference

U.S. Census Bureau, *Money Income in the United States: 1999* (P60–209), Washington, GPO, 2000, appendices A, D, and E.

3

The Income Density Function

The right-sided skewness of the U.S. household income distribution for 1999 shown in figures 2.1 and 2.2 is a pattern that has been observed in almost every country that has ever published income distribution data. The characteristic features are an asymmetric polygon with a long sloping right-sided tail. The left side of the polygon is dominated by a rounded peak whose top is over the lower income portion of the income axis.

In the late nineteenth century, Pareto took notice of the long sloping right-sided tail and postulated that all countries over all time periods could describe their income distribution with a statistical model that describes this tail. However, Pareto's Law did not take the rounded peak on the left-hand side of the distribution into consideration, and while his model subsequently proved to give a good description of the incomes of the more affluent households, it could not describe the incomes of the rest of the households, which are the bulk of the population.

3.1 Asymmetry in Income Distribution

Contributing Factors

The asymmetrical shape of the histogram and polygon are especially pronounced in developing countries. In a landmark research paper published in 1963, Simon Kuznets of Harvard University drew attention to the finding that "the shape of the income distribution curve is different in underdeveloped and developed countries. The low income groups of the former receive shares in total income as high as those of the low income groups in the developed countries; but the upper income brackets in the underdeveloped countries receive appreciably higher shares in total income than they do in developed

Table 3.1 Family Income in the Philippines, 1991

Income Class	Total Number of Families
Under P10,000	307
10,000–19,999	1,648
20,000–29,999	2,145
30,000–39,999	1,732
40,000–49,999	1,251
50,000–59,999	979
60,000–79,999	1,235
80,000–99,999	773
100,000–149,999	1,018
150,000–249,999	594
250,000–499,999	237
500,000 and over	60

Source: National Statistical Office, 1991 FIES, Manila, Philippines.

countries" [4]. Table 3.1 and figure 3.1 illustrate the case of the Republic of the Philippines. When table 3.1 is put into a histogram, it yields the rather skewed income distribution of figure 3.1.

The empirical evidence seems at first counterintuitive, mainly because it has been well established that all human traits—such as intelligence, diligence, and physical size—that might contribute to accruing income are normally distributed. That is, they are distributed symmetrically among the population. One would expect, then, that income distribution should also be symmetrical, rewarding those with the most income earning potential the highest incomes, whereas those with the least would earn the lowest incomes. In that case, the average household should be in the middle of the distribution, accruing the average income, and the average, modal, and median incomes would all be the same.

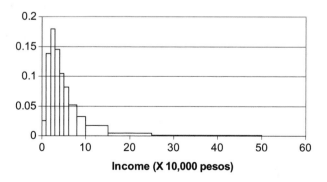

Figure 3.1. Philippines, 1991

However, if one reflects on the fact that in many countries (or perhaps all countries) income for most people is mainly derived from earnings, skew income distributions are not so surprising. For example, in the United States, 75% of the people who had income in 1998 had income from earnings, and this accounted for about 80% of all income. Furthermore, of those whose incomes did not currently contain earnings, many of them, such as pensioners and those on disability, had income that was based on past earnings.

Now microeconomics tells us that earnings are mostly related to the marginal revenue product of the skills employed, and as we know from table 1.1, skills that are education intensive generally command a higher marginal revenue product. But there is a pyramid effect in education that limits the number of people who reach those high levels of education that command higher earnings. While the earnings distributions across skills might have the same shape, the means of the distributions will be related to the educational/skill level of the group. Because of the pyramid effect, more people will find themselves in earnings distributions that have low and medium mean incomes than in distributions that have high mean incomes. When these distributions are combined over all skill levels, the final shape will be distorted into a skewed distribution.

3.2 Statistical Modeling

The Income Density Function

The skewness observed in income distribution survey data suggests that a probability density function be used to generate the descriptive statistics associated with income distribution. If a good-fitting probability model could be found for the survey, then a whole host of consistent statistics would be generated. The candidates for such a model should be single-mode, right-hand skewed density functions. It is also desirable to have a model whose cumulative distribution function (CDF) is invertible; that is, it has an inverse. This feature will allow the researcher to find the cut-off income levels associated with quantiles of the population. The goodness of fit will mainly depend on the number of fitting parameters. As we shall see in chapters 5 and 6, the models with four or five parameters generally give better fits than those with less parameters.

If we let $f(y)$ be our income density function, we define the probability of a randomly selected income unit as having an income between y_1 and y_2 as:

$$P(y_1 < y < y_2) = \int_{y_1}^{y_2} f(y)dy.$$

The above probability is the area under $f(y)$ between the incomes y_1 and y_2, as shown in figure 3.2.

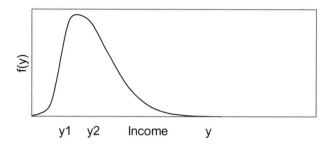

Figure 3.2. Income Density Function

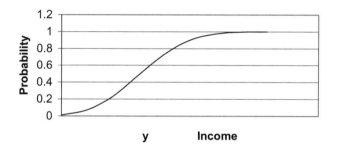

Figure 3.3. Cumulative Distribution Function

Likewise, the cumulative distribution is the probability of a randomly se-lected income unit having an income less than some income y, as shown in figure 3.3. That is,

$$F(y) = \int_0^y f(y)dy.$$

Example 1

A frequently used model for the income density function is the lognormal distribution given by the formula:

$$f(y) = \frac{1}{\sqrt{2\pi}\sigma} \frac{1}{y} e^{\frac{-(\ln y - \mu)^2}{2\sigma^2}}.$$

The underlying assumption for this model is that ln y has a normal distribution, which can be tested using a standard statistical test such as the chi-squared test. The parameters of the model, μ and σ, must be estimated for any particular set of data. The model is appealing because it can be transformed into a standard normal distribution through a simple substitution. That is, if we let

$$z = \frac{\ln y - \mu}{\sigma},$$

it follows that

$$dz = \frac{dy}{y\sigma}.$$

Hence,

$$F(y) = \int_0^y \frac{1}{\sqrt{2\pi}\sigma} \frac{1}{y} e^{\frac{-(\ln y - \mu)^2}{2\sigma^2}} dy,$$

which transforms into

$$F(z) = \int_{-\infty}^z \frac{1}{\sqrt{2\pi}} e^{\frac{-z^2}{2}} dz.$$

This is the cumulative distribution function of the standard normal, which makes it possible to use the standard normal tables found in the appendix of any statistical text to compute the probability of a sampling unit's income being between any two income levels. Alternatively, there is a computerized version of the standard normal tables that is included with many statistical software packages that is even more precise.

The mean of the lognormal is given by

$$\mu_y = e^{\mu + \frac{\sigma^2}{2}},$$

and the variance is given by

$$\sigma_y^2 = e^{2\mu + 2\sigma^2} - e^{2\mu + \sigma^2}.$$

When the mean and variance are estimated in the income distribution survey, μ and σ can be estimated in terms of μ_y and σ_y^2. That is,

$$\sigma^2 = \ln\left[\frac{\mu_y^2 + \sigma_y^2}{\mu_y^2}\right] \quad \text{and} \quad \mu = \ln \mu_y - \frac{\sigma^2}{2}.$$

Example 2

In order to illustrate the lognormal model, let us make use of the data given in table 3.2 from the U.S. Census Bureau report, *Money Income in the United States: 1999*. Although the Census Bureau estimates the mean, it does not give an estimate of the standard deviation. Instead, it estimates the standard error of the mean, which is a function of the standard deviation of the entire distribution, but it is impossible to extract the standard deviation from the standard error of the mean without knowing what weights were used. However, the standard deviation can be estimated using standard formulas for grouped data.

Table 3.2 Male Full-Time Year-Round Workers, 1999 (Numbers in Thousands of People)

Income Class Interval ($)	Number F	Proportion p	Class Midpoint x
1–5,000	698	0.012135	2,500
5,000–10,000	1,009	0.017542	7,500
10,000–15,000	3,217	0.055928	12,500
15,000–25,000	9,944	0.172879	20,000
25,000–35,000	10,712	0.186231	30,000
35,000–50,000	12,457	0.216568	42,500
50,000–75,000	10,914	0.189743	62,500
75,000 +	8,569	0.148974	
Total	57,520		
Mean Income $50,438			

Before we do that, however, we will have to make an estimate of the midpoint of the open-ended class; that is, the class where income is above $75,000. In the absence of any information about that class, we will use the mean income estimated by the Census Bureau ($\mu_y = 50,438$) to estimate total income. Therefore, total income equals the total population (of male full-time year-round workers) times the mean income; that is, total income equals 57,520 × $50,438 = $2,901,193,760. Now we can estimate the amount of income that flowed to the open-ended class by subtracting from the total income the income that flowed to the other classes, as shown below.

The number 1,119,881,260 in the last column of table 3.3 is obtained by subtracting the sum of all other class incomes from the total income. Note also that the class midpoints are estimates of the average income for that class, but

Table 3.3 Male Full-Time Year-Round Workers, 1999 (Numbers in Thousands of People)

Income Class Interval ($)	Number F	Class Midpoint x	Class Income $y = F \cdot x$
1–5,000	698	2,500	1,745,000
5,000–10,000	1,009	7,500	7,567,500
10,000–15,000	3,217	12,500	40,212,500
15,000–25,000	9,944	20,000	198,880,000
25,000–35,000	10,712	30,000	321,360,000
35,000–50,000	12,457	42,500	529,422,500
50,000–75,000	10,914	62,500	682,125,000
75,000 +	8,569	130,690	1,119,881,260
Total	57,520		2,901,193,760
Mean Income $50,438			

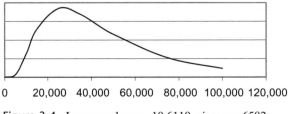

0   20,000 40,000 60,000 80,000 100,000 120,000

Figure 3.4. Lognormal mu $= 10.6119$, sigma $= .6582$

the open-ended class average income is obtained by dividing the total class income by the number in that class, that is, $130,690 = 1,119,881,260/8,569$.

To get the variance of the distribution, we will apply the formula:

$$\sigma_y^2 = \sum_{i=1}^{c} p_i x_i^2 - \mu_y^2,$$

where c is the number of classes, and the probabilities are estimated by the proportions in table 3.2. Applying this formula, we get a variance of 1,379,385,542 and a standard deviation of 37,140.08. Hence, we can now compute the parameters of the lognormal distribution using the formulas given in Example 1, as shown in table 3.3.

$$\sigma^2 = \ln\left[\frac{\mu_y^2 + \sigma_y^2}{\mu_y^2}\right] = \ln\left[\frac{50,438^2 + 37,140^2}{50,438^2}\right]$$

$$= \ln[1.542213036] = .433218421.$$

$$\mu = \ln \mu_y - \frac{\sigma^2}{2} = \ln(50,438) - \frac{.433218421}{2} = 10.61189093,$$

$$\sigma = \sqrt{.433218421} = .6581933.$$

The distribution for these parameters is shown in figure 3.4.

Example 3

We can use the lognormal model estimated in Example 2 to estimate the probability that a randomly chosen male (who is employed full-time and year-round) has an annual income between $40,000 and $60,000. To do this, let

$$z_1 = \frac{\ln(40,000) - 10.61189093}{.6581933}$$

and let

$$z_2 = \frac{\ln(60,000) - 10.61189093}{.6581933}$$

which yields $z_1 = -0.0231789$ and $z_2 = 0.5928485$.

Table 3.4 Female Full-Time Year-Round Workers, 1999 (Numbers in Thousands of People)

Income Class Interval ($)	Number F	Proportion p	Class Midpoint x
1–5,000	633	0.015660	2,500
5,000–10,000	1,391	0.034413	7,500
10,000–15,000	4,059	0.100418	12,500
15,000–25,000	11,049	0.273348	20,000
25,000–35,000	9,433	0.233369	30,000
35,000–50,000	7,656	0.189406	42,500
50,000–75,000	4,185	0.103535	62,500
75,000 +	2,015	0.049850	
Total	40,421		
Mean Income $33,303			

Source: U.S. Census Bureau, *Money Income in the United States: 1999* (P60–209), Washington, GPO, 2000.

From the standard normal tables we get .2326 as the probability of a full-time year-round male worker having an income between $40,000 and $60,000 a year. Since there are a total of 57,520 male full-time year-round workers in this sample, $.2326 \times 57,520 = 13,780$ are estimated to earn between $40,000 and $60,000 annually.

Problems

1. Consider table 3.4 for females who work full-time and year-round in 1999.
   a. Estimate μ_y and σ_y^2 for the table.
   b. Estimate the parameters μ and σ for the lognormal distribution.
   c. Estimate the probability that a randomly selected full-time year-round female worker will have an income between $40,000 and $60,000.
   d. Estimate the probability that a randomly selected *male* full-time year-round worker will have an annual income above $60,000. Compare this with the probability that a *female* full-time year-round worker will have an annual income above $60,000.
2. Show $\sigma^2 = \ln\left[\frac{\mu_y^2 + \sigma_y^2}{\mu_y^2}\right]$ and $\mu = \ln \mu_y - \frac{\sigma^2}{2}$.

The following problems are only recommended for students who have had an intermediate course in mathematical statistics.

1. Show that the parameters μ and σ of the lognormal are the mean and standard deviation of the $\ln y$. *Hint*: Find the mean and variance of $z = \frac{\ln y - \mu}{\sigma}$ using the expectation operator and the variance operator.

2. Show that $\mu_y = e^{\mu + \frac{\sigma^2}{2}}$ and $\sigma_y^2 = e^{2\mu + 2\sigma^2} - e^{2\mu + \sigma^2}$ *Hint*: Set $y^r = [e^{\mu + \sigma z}]^r = e^{r(\mu + \sigma z)}$ and find an expression for $E(y^r)$.

References

1. Aitchison, J. and J. A. Brown, *The Lognormal Distribution*, Cambridge, Cambridge University Press, 1957.
2. Gilbrat, R. *Les inégalités économique*, Paris, Siney, 1931.
3. Kakwani, Nanak C., *Income Inequality and Poverty*, Research Publication for the World Bank, Washington, Oxford University Press, 1980.
4. Kuznets, S., *Quantitative Aspects of the Economic Growth of Nations: Distribution of Income by Size*, Economic Development and Cultural Change, Vol. 11, No. 2, Pt. 2, Chicago, Chicago University Press, 1963, pp. 1–79.
5. Pareto, V., *Cours d'economique politique*, Rouge, Lausanne, 1897.

4

Goodness of Fit

In chapter 3 we saw how we could use the lognormal probability density function as a model of the male full-time year-round workers in the United States (1999) income distribution. The benefit of using a probability density function as a model of the income density function is that the generation of statistics about the population, such as means, medians, quantiles, and so forth, will be based upon their theoretical definitions as related to the density function. Hence they will be fully consistent with one another. The full significance of this will become clearer when we compute these statistics using alternative methods.

However, if the model does not describe the observed data well, it is possible to have fully consistent estimates that are not a good reflection of the reality. Therefore, income distribution researchers are concerned about finding models that "fit" the observed sample surveys as tightly as possible. They go about it in two steps: (1) Select a model. (2) Find the values of the parameters of the model that give the best fit. After they find the best-fitting parameters for a particular model, they start all over with another model and finally select the model that yields the best fit. In this chapter we will discus this procedure for the lognormal. In subsequent chapters, we will compare the lognormal to alternative models.

4.1 Measures of Goodness of Fit

Mean Absolute Deviation

This method of measuring the goodness of fit compares the number of sampling units (people, households, or families) predicted by the model with what was actually observed in the sample by computing the mean of the absolute

Table 4.1 Male Full-Time Year-Round Workers, 1999 (Numbers in Thousands of People): Computation of MAD for a Lognormal Distribution with mu = 10.61189093 and sigma = .6581933

Income Class ($)	Observed f_o	Estimated f_c	Abs. Diff. $\lvert f_o - f_c \rvert$
1–5,000	698	42	656
5,000–10,000	1,009	913	96
10,000–15,000	3,217	2,789	428
15,000–25,000	9,944	9,513	431
25,000–35,000	10,712	10,359	353
35,000–50,000	12,457	12,273	184
50,000–75,000	10,914	11,525	611
75,000 +	8,569	10,106	1,537
Total	57,520	57,520	4,296

MAD = 4,296/8 = 537

deviations. The formula for computing the mean absolute deviation (MAD) is given by:

$$\text{MAD} = \frac{\sum_1^{n_c} \lvert f_o - f_c \rvert}{n_c},$$

where for each income class:

f_o = the number of sampling units observed,
f_c = the number of sampling units estimated by the model, and
n_c = the number of income classes.

The calculation of MAD for male full-time year-round workers in 1999 is shown in table 4.1

Mean Squared Error

This measure differs from MAD in that it squares the differences before adding them up. In doing so, it gives more weight to the large errors than to the small errors. The formula is given by:

$$\text{MSE} = \frac{\sum_1^{n_c} (f_o - f_c)^2}{n_c}.$$

The calculation of MSE for male full-time year-round workers in 1999 is shown in table 4.2

Chi-squared Statistic

Perhaps the most commonly computed statistic, the chi-squared statistic (CHISQ) is computationally not much different than the mean squared error.

Table 4.2 Male Full-Time Year-Round Workers, 1999 (Numbers in Thousands of People): Computation of MES for a Lognormal Distribution with mu $= 10.61189093$ and sigma $= .6581933$

Income Class ($)	Observed f_0	Estimated f_c	Sqr. Diff. $(f_0 - f_c)^2$
1–5,000	698	42	430,336
5,000–10,000	1,009	913	9,216
10,000–15,000	3,217	2,789	183,184
15,000–25,000	9,944	9,513	185,761
25,000–35,000	10,712	10,359	124,609
35,000–50,000	12,457	12,273	33,856
50,000–75,000	10,914	11,525	373,321
75,000 +	8,569	10,106	2,362,369
Total	57,520	57,520	3,702,652

MSE $= 3,702,652/8 = 462,831.5$

In many cases, the minimum chi-squared and the maximum likelihood estimates are identical [1]. The computed squared error for each income class is divided by the frequency computed for the class before it is summed. This gives an approximation to a sum of normal Z distributions squared, which is the definition of the chi-squared distribution. The formula is given below:

$$\text{CHISQ} = \sum_{1}^{n_c} \frac{(f_o - f_c)^2}{f_c}.$$

Table 4.3 shows the calculation of CHISQ.

Table 4.3 Male Full-Time Year-Round Workers, 1999 (Numbers in Thousands of People): Computation of CHISQ for a Lognormal Distribution with mu $= 10.61189093$ and sigma $= .6581933$

Income Class ($)	Observed f_0	Estimated f_c	$(f_0 - f_c)^2/f_c$
1–5,000	698	42	10,246.095
5,000–10,000	1,009	913	10.094
10,000–15,000	3,217	2,789	65.681
15,000–25,000	9,944	9,513	19.527
25,000–35,000	10,712	10,359	12.029
35,000–50,000	12,457	12,273	2.759
50,000–75,000	10,914	11,525	32.392
75,000 +	8,569	10,106	233.759
Total	57,520	57,520	10,622.3

CHISQ $= 10,622.3$

Table 4.4 Male Full-Time Year-Round Workers, 1999 (Numbers in Thousands of People): Computation of the K-S Statistic for a Lognormal Distribution with mu = 10.61189093 and sigma = .6581933

Income Class ($)	Observed F_0	Estimated F_c	Abs. Diff. $|F_0 - F_c|$
1–5,000	.012	.007	.005
5,000–10,000	.030	.017	.013
10,000–15,000	.086	.065	.021
15,000–25,000	.258	.230	.028
25,000–35,000	.445	.411	.034
35,000–50,000	.661	.624	.037*
50,000–75,000	.851	.824	.027
75,000+	1.000	1.000	

*K-S = .037

Note: The cumulative probabilities are computed from the cumulative observed and computed frequencies divided by the total population; that is, .012 = 698/57,520 and .007 = 42/57,520. Likewise, .030 = (698 + 913)/57,520, and so on.

Source: U.S. Census Bureau, Money Income in the United States: 1999 (P60–209), Washington, GPO, 2000.

The Kolmogorov-Smirnov Statistic

This statistic compares the computed cumulative density function (CDF) probabilities with the observed cumulative proportions. The largest absolute difference of these is the Kolmogorov-Smirnov (K-S) statistic. Mathematically, it is given by the following:

$$K\text{-}S = \sup|F_o(y) - F_c(y)|,$$

where "sup" is shorthand for the largest absolute difference. Table 4.4 shows the calculations of K-S.

4.2 The Direct-Search Method of Parameter Estimation

Optimizing the Fit Using the Chi-squared Statistic

Computers allow the income distribution researcher to optimize the fit of the income density model through the use of direct-search numerical techniques. The general principle involved is to write a computer program that will change the parameters of a model until some fit criterion is minimized. Accompanying this text is a program called *lognorm*, which will do a direct search for the parameters of a lognormal distribution by minimizing the chi-squared statistic. The program requires that the sample survey be input (in grouped data form) and an initial estimate of the parameters. The chi-squared statistic was selected as the measure to minimize because it can be interpreted as a generalized least-squares [2].

Our program starts by prompting for a reasonable solution for μ and σ. It checks the chi-squared value of the initial solution and then begins to incrementally change μ while holding σ constant. Each time a new value of μ is introduced, a computation of chi-squared is made and compared with the last value of chi-squared. If the new chi-squared is lower than the previous chi-squared, μ is replaced by the new value. This continues until the chi-squared value can no longer be lowered. At that point σ is incrementally changed while holding μ constant, replacing σ each time the chi-squared value goes down until the chi-squared can no longer be lowered. Then, once again, μ is changed while holding σ constant, and the process keeps repeating itself until the chi-squared value converges to some minimum point.

Table 4.5 illustrates how the values were replaced for the 1999 male full-time year-round workers data from chapter 3. Note the initial values of the parameters are the values we computed in chapter 3.

We see from table 4.5 that a relatively minor change in the parameters can yield a rather large change in the chi-squared statistic. For this reason in judging the fit of a distribution it is prudent to look at more than one fit statistic. In table 4.6 we compare all four fit statistics for the initial and least chi-square values of μ and σ.

The results summarized in table 4.6 give mixed signals. While the least chi-squared parameters show a substantial reduction in the chi-squared statistic, all other fit statistics favor using the initial parameters. To get another idea of the difference between these two fits, it is useful to see their graphs.

Visually, the graph in figure 4.1 seems to fit a little better than the one in figure 4.2 If given a choice between the two fits, most people would be inclined to choose the graph in figure 4.1 which is drawn from the initial estimates of the parameters. However, as we shall see in chapter 5, there are alternative models to the lognormal that might fit better than either of these.

Problems

1. Using the parameters of the lognormal distribution estimated for female full-time year-round workers, 1999 (from problem 1, chapter 3), compute the MAD, MSE, CHISQ, and K-S statistics.
2. Find a pair of the least chi-squared lognormal parameters for female full-time year-round workers, 1999 using the *lognorm* program.
3. Construct a table like table 4.6 for the initial and least chi-squared parameters for female full-time year-round workers, 1999.

Table 4.5 Minimizing Chi-squared for the Lognormal
Male Full-Time Year-Round Workers, 1999

Mu	Sigma	Chi-squared
	Initial Values	
10.6119	0.658193	10,622.3
	Changed Values	
10.5119	.658193	5,926.3
10.4119	.658193	5,614.0
10.4219	.658193	5,471.3
10.4319	.658193	5,366.1
10.4419	.658193	5,298.6
10.4519	.658193	5,269.4
10.4529	.658193	5,268.6
10.4539	.658193	5,268.2
10.4549	.658193	5,268.1
10.4549	.737713	2,911.0
10.4549	.758193	3,002.6
10.4549	.748193	2,936.1
10.4549	.738193	2,911.2
10.4549	.737893	2,911.1
10.4549	.737713	2,911.0
10.5549	.737713	2,887.4
10.5449	.737713	2,791.9
10.5349	.737713	2,718.8
10.5249	.737713	2,667.5
10.5149	.737713	2,638.1
10.5049	.737713	2,630.3
10.5059	.737713	2,630.1
10.5059	.747713	2,622.6
10.5059	.746713	2,621.1
10.5059	.745713	2,620.0
10.5059	.744713	2,619.5
10.5059	.743713	2,619.4
10.5059	.744193	2,619.4
10.5069	.744193	2,618.8
10.5079	.744193	2,618.4
10.5089	.744193	2,618.2
10.5089	.744593	2,618.2

Table 4.6 A Comparison between the Initial and Least
Chi-squared Values of Mu and Sigma

Parameters	MAD	MSE	CHISQ	K-S	
μ: 10.6119	537	462,831.5	10,622.3	.037	σ: 0.658193
μ: 10.5089	1046.8	1,204,479.0	2,618.2	.044	σ: 0.744593

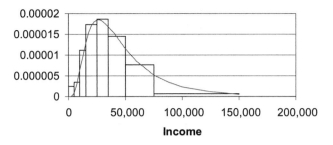

Figure 4.1. Lognormal mu = 10.6119, sigma = .6582

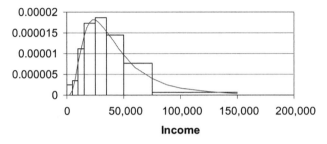

Figure 4.2. Lognormal mu = 10.5089, sigma = .7446

References

1. Berkson, J., *Maximum Likelihood and Minimum Chi-squared Estimates of the Logistic Function*, American Statistical Association Journal, March 1955, pp. 130–161.
2. Kloek, T. and H. K. Van Dijk, *Efficient Estimation of Income Distribution Parameters*, Journal of Econometrics 8, 1978, pp. 61–74.

Supplement to Chapter 4

Using a Spreadsheet to Graph the Income Density Fit

Figures 4.1 and 4.2 as well as the other graphs of income distributions presented in this text were drawn using a standard spreadsheet. In this case, *Microsoft EXCEL* was used, but the technique presented here is similar to what must be done in other software packages. There are some advantages to using a spreadsheet to draw the distributions. For one, spreadsheets are almost universally available; thus many people are familiar with their usage. Also, the graphs can be transferred to other standard software packages, such as word processors. However, the most important reason is because spreadsheets allow the user to input the equation of the fitted density function to compute the coordinates of the

Table 4.7 Male Full-Time Year-Round Workers, 1999 (Numbers in Thousands of People): Computation of Areas and Heights for Histogram

Income Class ($)	f_0	Prob.	Height
1–5,000	698	.0121349	.000000242746
5,000–10,000	1,009	.0175417	.000000350834
10,000–15,000	3,217	.0559283	.000001118560
15,000–25,000	9,944	.1728290	.000001728790
25,000–35,000	10,712	.1862308	.000001862300
35,000–50,000	12,457	.2165681	.000001443780
50,000–75,000	10,914	.1897427	.000000758970
75,000+–(186,380)	8,569	.1489742	.000000133753
Total	57,520	1.000000	

fitted graph, thereby yielding a picture that shows accurately the difference between the fitted density function and the sample survey histogram.

We will begin by drawing the graph of the sample survey histogram. For our purposes, we need to draw histograms whose areas represent probabilities of falling between two income levels. These are computed by dividing the frequency of observed for the income class by the total in the sample, as shown in table 4.7. In the $10,000 to $15,000 income class, for example, the frequency observed is 3,217; hence the probability of being in that income bracket is $3,217/57,520 = .0559283$. To determine the height of each income class, divide the probability of being in that income class by the width of the income class (the width is the difference between the endpoints of the class). For example, the height of the income class $10,000 to $15,000 is $.0559283/(15,000 - 10,000) = .00001118566$.

For the purpose of getting a height for the open-ended class—$75,000+ in this case—we will close that class with an estimate of a ceiling income based on the average income for the class, $130,690 (see Example 2, chapter 3). To do this, we let x be the ceiling income; then

$$(x + 750,000)/2 = 130,690,$$

and solving for x we get $x = \$186,380$. Hence the width of the last class is estimated to be $186,380 - 75,000 = 111,380$.

We are now ready to enter data into a spreadsheet to draw the histogram. The data will appear in a spreadsheet as shown in table 4.8 The heights for each income class were entered as shown in table 4.7 but were converted to scientific notation by *EXCEL*. You will notice that the income class endpoints were entered three times, except for the first and last, which were entered twice. The reason for that is because the graph software that was selected was *SCATTER-line*, which draws lines from one coordinate pair to another co-ordinate pair. Hence, for each income class rectangle we need a point on the left bottom of the rectangle and a point above it at the height of the rectangle. These two points define the left vertical side of the rectangle.

Table 4.8 Spreadsheet for Histogram

Y	Height	Direction
1	0	left bottom of class 1–5,000
1	2.42746E-07	height of class 1–5,000
5,000	2.42746E-07	
5,000	0	left bottom of class 5,000–10,000
5,000	3.50834E-07	height of class 5,000–10,000
10,000	3.50834E-07	
10,000	0	left bottom of class 10,000–15,000
10,000	1.11856E-06	height of class 10,000–15,000
15,000	1.11856E-06	
15,000	0	left bottom of class 15,000–25,000
15,000	1.72879E-06	height of class 15,000–25,000
25,000	1.72879E-06	
25,000	0	left bottom of class 25,000–35,000
25,000	1.8623E-06	height of class 25,000–35,000
35,000	1.8623E-06	
35,000	0	etc.
35,000	1.44378E-06	
50,000	1.44378E-06	
50,000	0	
50,000	7.5897E-07	
75,000	7.5897E-07	
75,000	0	
75,000	1.33753E-07	
186,380	1.33753E-07	
186,380	0	

Next, we move from the left side to the right side of the rectangle along the top, and down from the top to the bottom of the rectangle. That completes the rectangle for one class, and the next rectangle is started by drawing a line above the right-side income of the last income class to the height of the next income class. This yields the left verticle side of the next rectangle. The process continues until all rectangles are drawn.

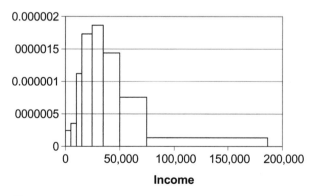

Figure 4.3. Male Full-Time Year-Round Workers, 1999

Table 4.9 Spreadsheet for Histogram and Fitted Curve

Y	Height	$f(y)$
1	0	2.17376E-57
1	0.000002426	2.17376E-57
2,500	0.000002426	3.0828E-08
5,000	0.000002426	7.6606E-07
5,000	0	7.6606E-07
5,000	0.000003508	7.6606E-07
7,500	0.000003508	3.00052E-06
10,000	0.000003508	6.27972E-06
10,000	0	6.27972E-06
10,000	0.000011185	6.27972E-06
12,500	0.000011185	9.76325E-06
15,000	0.000011185	1.28568E-05
15,000	0	1.28568E-05
15,000	0.000017287	1.28568E-05
17,500	0.000017287	1.52828E-05
20,000	0.000017287	1.69816E-05
22,500	0.000017287	1.80101E-05
25,000	0.000017287	1.84747E-05
25,000	0	1.84747E-05
25,000	0.000018623	1.84747E-05
27,500	0.000018623	1.84926E-05
30,000	0.000018623	1.81731E-05
35,000	0.000018623	1.68805E-05
35,000	0	1.68805E-05
35,000	0.000014437	1.68805E-05
40,000	0.000014437	1.51487E-05
45,000	0.000014437	1.33067E-05
50,000	0.000014437	1.15325E-05
50,000	0	1.15325E-05
50,000	0.000007589	1.15325E-05
60,000	0.000007589	8.47393E-06
75,000	0.000007589	5.23517E-06
75,000	0	5.23517E-06
75,000	2.67506E-07	5.23517E-06
87,500	2.67506E-07	3.50988E-06
100,000	2.67506E-07	2.37479E-06
125,000	2.67506E-07	1.12772E-06
186,380	2.67506E-07	9.58765E-07
186,380	0	9.58765E-07

The spreadsheet is table 4.8 produced the graph shown in figure 4.3.

In order to draw the fitted curve around the histogram, a third column must be introduced to the spreadsheet, which is computed from the formula of the lognormal using the estimated values of μ and σ. The modified spreadsheet is shown in table 4.9.

The numbers in the third column were obtained by inserting the income density function as a function for the column. In *EXCEL*, the function is

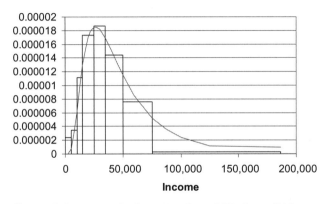

Figure 4.4. Male Full-Time Year-Round Workers, 1999

specified in the first cell of the third column as:

$$= \exp(-((\ln(A2) - 10.6119)^2)/.866448)/(A2 * .164986273),$$

and then the formula is "dragged down" the column to get all the rest of the numbers. Additional points were added to give the fitted curve more definition. These can be added arbitrarily in the income class around the mode of the distribution and other places where the function is less linear. Note, $2\sigma\sigma = 2(.6582)(.6582) = .86645448$, and the square root of two pi sigma is equal to .164986273, when sigma is equal to .6582. This spreadsheet will produce the graph shown in figure 4.4.

5

Alternative Income Density Models

The lognormal income distribution density model that we have been using was introduced by Gibrat [6] in 1931. For many years, it was the model of choice for income distribution studies, but it has a history of not being able to sufficiently describe the upper and lower tails of the income density function. It had as a predecessor the Pareto [8] distribution, which was an excellent model of incomes above average income, that is, the upper tail, but deficient in describing the income distribution for the rest of the population.

In 1952, Champernowne [3] presented two more models, the four- and five-parameter formulas, which were a further elaboration of a family of models that he proposed in 1937. These models used the Pareto model for the upper tail and were able to capture the shape that was necessary to describe the rest of the population. However, in order to achieve this flexibility, more parameters were necessary, and this made fitting these models difficult.

In a sense, the Champernowne models were a little ahead of their time because computer usage was not as common in 1952 as it was 10 years later. As more economists gained access to computers, the problem of parameter estimation became less difficult, and more models were introduced. Among some of the more well known ones are the sech^2 distribution introduced by Fisk [6] in 1961, the Beta model by Thurow [13] in 1970, the Gamma model by Salem and Mount [10] in 1974, the new model by Dagum [4] in 1975, the Weibull distribution by Bartels and van Metelen [1] in 1975, the Singh-Maddala [11] model in 1976, and the log-logistic model.

In all of these models, emphasis is on describing the historical income distribution as accurately as possible. There are several good reasons for this. For one, the fitted distribution can be used to estimate the probability of an income recipient being between *any* two income levels. As mentioned in earlier chapters, a fitted continuous distribution will allow the researcher to estimate a consistent set of income summary statistics for the population. Also, the parameters of many of these models have an economic interpretation. However, not all parameters do, and while they may have an economic interpretation, no model at this time has a set of parameters that can be predicted by macroeconomic fiscal and/or monetary policy. Hopefully, sometime in the twenty-first century this will be done.

In this chapter we will focus on a few of these models, namely, the log-logistic, the Singh-Maddala, the Dagum, and the Champernowne five-parameter formulas. These have been selected because they have been tested on the income distribution surveys of over 100 countries at the United Nations and have proven to give good fits. Another reason for selecting this group is that they have cumulative distribution functions that are easy to work with because they can be expressed as algebraic formulas and because they have inverses. However, one should not automatically dismiss the other models mentioned above. It is possible that you may find a summary table that cannot be fit by one of the four chosen for this chapter, and the best fit is with the Beta or the Gamma or one of the other distributions omitted in this chapter. Microcomputers and the efficient estimation techniques proposed by Kloek and Van Dijk [8] make practically all models an alternative option today.

5.1 The Log-logistic Model

Income Density Function

Camilo Dagum [4] of the University of Ottawa drew attention to this model when he used it to analyze the income distribution of Canada and several subregions of the country. The fits were surprisingly good for a two-parameter model. In a later study, Terukazu Suruga [12] of Osaka University showed how the log-logistic fit better than the lognormal, Gamma, and Beta distributions for a time series of Japanese income distributions. Its fit was comparable to the Singh-Maddala distribution, which requires one more parameter to estimate.

The density function is specified by:

$$f(y) = \frac{e^{\frac{\ln y - m}{k}}}{ky\left[e^{\frac{\ln y - m}{k}} + 1\right]^2},$$

where m is ln (median income) and $k > 0$ is a scale parameter. We will fit the distribution by first finding a reasonable approximation for the median income and inputting it into the *loglog* program. To find an estimate of the median income, we will use the procedure shown in table 5.1.

Table 5.1 Male Full-Time Year-Round Workers, 1999
(Numbers in Thousands of People): Rough Estimate
of the Median Income

Income Class ($)	f_0	Cumulative f_0
1–5,000	698	698
5,000–10,000	1,009	1,707
10,000–15,000	3,217	4,924
15,000–25,000	9,944	14,868
25,000–35,000	10,712	25,580
35,000–50,000	12,457	38,037 ← 28,751
50,000–75,000	10,914	—
75,000+	8,569	—
Total	57,520	

Note: The median occurs for the $57,520/2 = 28,751$ sampling unit.
This lies in the income class $35,000 to $50,000. Any income in this
range would be a reasonable estimate of the median income–be used
with the direct-search software package *loglog*.

One can get a very close estimate of the median income and reduce the
number of iterations it takes to converge on the estimated parameters by applying the elementary formula for estimating the median from grouped data.

$$m = L + \frac{(\frac{n}{2} - \sum_1^{i-1} f_0)(U - L)}{f_{0_1}}.$$

Here L is the lower limit of the income class containing the median income.

U is the upper limit of the same income class.

n is the total sample size.

f_{0_1} is the number of sampling units in that class.

Substituting these values from table 5.1 into the equation we get:

$$M = 35,000 + [(28,751 - 25,580)/12,457](50,000 - 35,000)$$
$$= 35,000 + (3,171/12,457)15,000$$
$$= 35,000 + 3,818.3351$$
$$= 38,818.3351.$$

Hence, the estimate of the median income is 38,818.

When 38,818 is input into *loglog* with the above data for male full-time
year-round workers, 1999 the fit in table 5.2 is obtained. As we can see in table
5.2, the fit statistics obtained for the log-logistic are far better than what could
be obtained with the lognormal.

Furthermore, careful inspection of the fit shown in figure 5.1 reveals how
much better the log-logistic fits the upper tail of this distribution than the
lognormal. One of the main problems with the lognormal is the difficulty in
fitting the tails of most income distribution sample surveys.

Table 5.2 Male Full-Time Year-Round Workers, 1999 (Numbers in Thousands of People): Computation of MAD, MSE, CHISQ, and K-S for a Log-logistic Distribution with $m = 10.544$ and $k = .40363$

	Observed	Estimated	Pc. diff.
Income Class ($)	f_0	f_c	% Error
1–5,000	698	377	−46.0
5,000–10,000	1,009	1,662	64.7
10,000–15,000	3,217	3,208	−0.3
15,000–25,000	9,944	9,850	−0.9
25,000–35,000	10,712	10,803	0.9
35,000–50,000	12,457	12,331	−1.0
50,000–75,000	10,914	10,319	−5.5
75,000+	8,569	8,970	4.7
Total	57,520	57,520	

MAD = 286.3, MSE = 134,668.8, CHISQ = 585.1, K-S = .0069

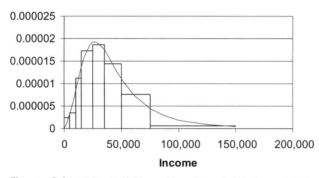

Figure 5.1. Male Full-Time Year-Round Workers, 1999: Log-logistic $m = 10.544$, $k = .40363$

Cumulative Distribution Function

The cumulative distribution function for the log-logistic is given by:

$$F(y) = 1 - \left[e^{\frac{\ln y - m}{k}} + 1 \right]^{-1}.$$

We can use the cumulative distribution function to compute the probability of being above or below a certain income, or the probability of being between two incomes, or it can find the income corresponding to some probability.

Example 1

Find the probability that a randomly selected male full-time year-round worker will havel an annual income below $80,000.

$$F(80{,}000) = 1 - \left[e^{\frac{\ln 80{,}000 - 10.544}{.40363}} + 1 \right]^{-1}$$
$$= 1 - \left[e^{\frac{.7457819}{.40363}} + 1 \right]^{-1} = 1 - [7.3451263]^{-1}$$
$$= .8639$$

Example 2

Find the probability that a randomly selected male full-time year-round worker will have an annual income between $60,000 and $80,000.

$$F(80{,}000) = .8639 \text{ and } F(60{,}000) = .5967; \text{ hence}$$
$$P(60{,}000 \leq y \leq 80{,}000) = .8639 - .5967 = .2672.$$

Example 3

What is the income at the 95th percentile for male full-time year-round workers? To do this we will use the inverse of the cumulative distribution function:

$$y = e^{k \ln \left(\frac{F(y)}{1-F(y)} \right) + m}.$$

Substituting .95 for $F(y)$ in the inverse and setting $k = .40363$ and $m = 10.544$, we get $y = \$124{,}550.17$. That is, only 5% of males in this category have an income above $124,550.17.

5.2 Singh-Maddala Model

Income Density Function

The Singh-Maddala [11] is a three-parameter model, thereby somewhat more adaptive to income sample surveys than the lognormal and log-logistic two-parameter models that we have so far studied. It is difficult to give the parameters an economic interpretation, but the model always gives good fits, though not necessarily the best fit of the four models that are discussed in this chapter.

Our direct-search algorithm developed for this model assumes that the user does not have an idea what a good set of initial values for these parameters should be and will assign them arbitrarily. In some cases this may lead to convergence on a local minimum. If that seems to be the case, then the user is advised to copy the last set of parameters estimated and to restart the search, inputting the last set of parameters slightly changed, and see if it converges to a lower chi-squared.

Table 5.3 Male Full-Time Year-Round Workers, 1999 (Numbers in Thousands of People): Computation of MAD, MSE, CHISQ, and K-S for the Singh-Maddala Distribution: $a_1 = .27756 \times 10^{-16}$, $a_2 = 3.8017$, $a_3 = .398$

Income Class($)	Observed f_0	Estimated f_c	Pc. Diff. % error
1–5,000	698	73	−89.5
5,000–10,000	1,009	919	−8.9
10,000–15,000	3,217	3,188	−0.9
15,000–25,000	9,944	13,110	31.8
25,000–35,000	10,712	12,458	16.3
35,000–50,000	12,457	10,744	−13.8
50,000–75,000	10,914	7,669	−29.7
75,000 +	8,569	9,358	9.2
Total	57,520	57,520	

MAD = 1,425, MSE = 3,444,819, CHISQ = 8,082, K-S = .0725

The income density function is specified as follows:

$$f(y) = a_1 a_2 a_3 \frac{y^{a_2-1}}{(1 + a_1 y^{a_2})^{a_3+1}}.$$

Obviously, none of these parameters may equal 0, since that would mean $f(y)$ would always be 0. However, they may be so close to 0, if it seems that they are 0.

When we input our data for male full-time year-round workers, 1999, we get the fit in table 5.3. The high-fit statistics as compared to the log-logistic and the lognormal are an indication that the direct-search routine converged on a local minimum. A rerun of the program setting $a_1 = .01$, $a_2 = 3.8$, and $a_3 = .4$ yields the fit in table 5.4.

Table 5.4 Male Full-Time Year-Round Workers, 1999 (Numbers in Thousands of People): Computation of MAD, MSE, CHISQ, and K-S for the Singh-Maddala Distribution $a_1 = .29112 \times 10^{-10}$, $a_2 = 2.2541$, $a_3 = 1.422$

Income Class ($)	Observed f_0	Estimated f_c	Pc. Diff. % error
1–5,000	698	514	−26.3
5,000–10,000	1,009	1,871	85.4
10,000–15,000	3,217	3,264	1.5
15,000–25,000	9,944	9,435	−5.1
25,000–35,000	10,712	10,398	−2.9
35,000–50,000	12,457	12,510	0.4
50,000–75,000	10,914	11,030	1.1
75,000 +	8,569	8,498	−0.8
Total	57,520	57,520	

MAD = 269.4, MSE = 144,669, CHISQ = 502, K-S = .0126

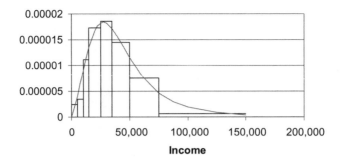

Figure 5.2. Male Full-Time Year-Round Workers, 1999: Singh-Maddala $a_1 = .29112 \times 10^{-10}$, $a_2 = 2.2541$, $a_3 = 1.422$

Not only do the fit statistics and the percentage error indicate a good fit; the graph in figure 5.2 shows how the fit looks.

Cumulative Distribution Function

It is easily verified by differentiation that the CDF for the Singh-Maddala is given by:

$$F(y) = 1 - (1 + a_1 y^{a_2})^{-a_3}.$$

If we let $p = F(y)$, then the inverse of the CDF can be expressed as:

$$y = \left\{ \frac{\left[\frac{1}{1-p}\right]^{\frac{1}{a_3}} - 1}{a_1} \right\}^{\frac{1}{a_2}}.$$

Example 4

Use the Singh-Maddala model to find the income at the 20th percentile for male full-time year-round workers. The 20% of males with the lowest incomes fall below this level (also called the bottom 20%).

$$y = \left\{ \frac{\left[\frac{1}{1-.2}\right]^{\frac{1}{1.422}} - 1}{.29112 \times 10^{-10}} \right\}^{\frac{1}{2.2541}}$$

$$y = \left\{ \frac{1.25^{.7032348} - 1}{.29112 \times 10^{-10}} \right\}^{.44366} = \$21,508.$$

5.3 A Four-Parameter Model—The Dagum

Income Density Function

Since its introduction in 1977 [5] the Dagum model has been used on almost every country that produces income distribution data. Research at the United Nations found that the Dagum was the model of choice for over 60 countries. It fit the Republic of Philippines income distribution so snugly that the National Economic and Development Authority (co-sponsored by the United Nations Development Programme) there launched a highly successful project called the Dagum Project, which attacked the pervasive poverty problem in the Philippines by first analyzing the income distribution of the 12 major regions of the country with the Dagum model and then formulating the basis of macroeconomic policy to combat the problem.

Dagum arrived at the model by first postulating a set of assumptions based on observed regularities found in empirical income distribution research. The four basic assumptions are:

A.1 Empirical income distributions are, in general, unimodal and positively (right-hand) skewed.

A.2 There exists a finite percentage of economic units with nil or negative income. If the economic units are composed of unattached individuals, this percentage corresponds to those unemployed unattached individuals without any source of income (social insurance, etc.) and proprietors with net losses. If the economic units are families with two or more members, they receive the same interpretation as unattached individuals, however this is the income of all members of the family units.

A.3 The income range is the closed-open interval $[y_0, \infty]$, where $y_0 > 0$, when the population of economic units is integrated with the employed members of the labour force. That is, the income distribution starts from the right of the origin, since it is composed of economic units with positive income. . . . It is also the case of the population of economic units obtained after elimination of its members with 0 or negative income.

A.4 The income elasticity of the cumulative distribution function $F(y)$, with respect to the origin α *of* $F(y)$, $\alpha < 1$, is a monotonic decreasing function of $F(y)$. This elasticity converges to a finite and positive value $\beta\delta$ when income y tends to 0; and it converges to 0 when income y tends to infinity. That is, for a given constant proportional rate of growth of income, there corresponds a decreasing proportional rate of growth of the cumulative distribution function $F(y)$, which depends on the size of $F(y)$ itself.

The above assumptions generate a differential equation that will set up a CDF whose density function is given by:

$$f(y) = \alpha, \Leftrightarrow y = 0,$$
$$f(y) = (1-\alpha)\lambda\beta\delta \cdot y^{-\delta-1}(1 + \lambda \cdot y^{-\delta})^{-\beta-1}, \Leftrightarrow y > 0,$$
$$f(y) = 0, \Leftrightarrow y < 0,$$

Table 5.5 Male Full-Time Year-Round Workers, 1999 (Numbers in Thousands of People): Computation of MAD, MSE, CHISQ, and K-S for the Dagum Distribution: $\alpha = .35946 \times 10^{-06}$, $\beta = .83441$, $\lambda = 23{,}008$, $\delta = 2.685$

	Observed	Estimated	Pc. Diff.
Income Class ($)	f_0	f_c	% error
1–5,000	698	484	−30.6
5,000–10,000	1,009	1,770	75.4
10,000–15,000	3,217	3,155	−1.9
15,000–25,000	9,944	9,461	−4.8
25,000–35,000	10,712	10,679	−0.3
35,000–50,000	12,457	12,689	1.9
50,000–75,000	10,914	10,739	−1.6
75,000 +	8,569	8,543	−0.3
Total	57,520	57,520	

MAD = 248.3, MSE = 118,533, CHISQ = 455, K–S = .0095

where the parameters have the following properties: $\beta\delta > 1$ implies the distribution is unimodal; if $0 < \beta\delta \leq 1$, then the distribution is nonmodal. And $0 \leq \alpha < 1$ is implied by assumption A.2, where α may be interpreted as the pure rate of unemployment for the case when $y_0 = 0$, and the majority of those unemployed are those without social insurance. $\lambda > 0$ is an antilog of the constant of integration. Inputting our data for male full-time year-round workers, 1999, we get the results shown in table 5.5 and figure 5.3.

As seen in table 5.5 the extra parameter in the Dagum tightens the fit even further for these data.

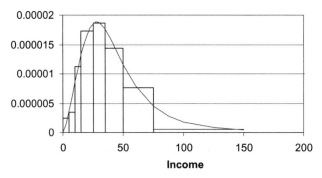

Figure 5.3. Male Full-Time Year-Round Workers, 1999: Dagum $\alpha = .35946 \times 10^{-6}$, $\beta = .83441$, $\lambda = 23{,}008$, $\delta = 2.685$

Cumulative Distribution Function

The Dagum CDF is given by:

$$F(y) = \alpha + \frac{1 - \alpha}{(1 + \lambda \cdot y^{-\delta})^{\beta}}, \lambda > 0.$$

The inverse of the CDF for any probability p is:

$$y = \lambda^{1/\delta} \left[\left(\frac{1 - \alpha}{p - \alpha} \right)^{1/\beta} - 1 \right]^{1/\delta}, p > \alpha.$$

5.4 The Champernowne Five-Parameter Formula

Income Density Function

When Champernowne [3] presented the five-parameter formula in 1952, the state of the art of computer technology at that time could be compared to the state of the art of printing technology the day after the invention of the printing press. There was very limited access to computers by anyone except the military, and using them was extremely tedious. In fact, even electronic handheld calculators were not yet invented. This was somewhat unfortunate because in the same paper Champernowne also presented a four-parameter model, which for the times was more practical and hence more commonly used. However, in the 1980s, experiments with both the four- and five-parameter formulas at the United Nations found that the five-parameter model gave much better fits. In actuality, only four of the five parameters have to be estimated; one parameter is the total number of income recipients, which is obtained from the sample.

When compared to the Dagum, the five-parameter formula gives comparable fits (see Campano [2]). It is always prudent to compute *both* of these models for the same sample survey because one serves as a check on the other. The density function is more complicated than the other models that we have looked at, not only because of the extra parameter but also because it has two functional forms, one for lower incomes and one for higher incomes.

Areas under this curve represent the probable number of sampling units that may have an income between income levels y_1 and y_2. It is given by:

$$f(y) = \frac{2N\alpha\sigma \sin \theta \left(\frac{y}{y_0} \right)^{\psi}}{y(1 + \sigma)\theta \left\{ 1 + 2\cos \theta \left(\frac{y}{y_0} \right)^{\psi} + \left(\frac{y}{y_0} \right)^{2\psi} \right\}},$$

where

$$\psi = \begin{cases} \alpha\sigma \leftrightarrow y \leq y_0 \\ \alpha \leftrightarrow y > y_0 \end{cases}$$

While the above income density is formidable, it is programmable and in today's personal computer environment a much more feasible model than in 1952. The parameter N is the size of the sample, which in the case of male full-time year-round workers, 1999 is 57,520. θ is used for adjusting the kurtosis or top of the frequency distribution. It must be given in radians and not in degrees. α is an estimate of the slope of the curve on the upper income side, also known as the Pareto constant for the population. The Latin parameter, y_0, is the mode of the income flow density distribution $g(y) = yf(y)$. Note that the mean income for any model is given by:

$$\mu_y = \int_{-\infty}^{\infty} yf(y)dy = \int_{-\infty}^{\infty} g(y)dy.$$

The fifth parameter σ is related to the skewness of the distribution, which describes the logarithm of income. In principle, σ should have a value close to 1.

Table 5.6 and figure 5.4 shows how the Champernowne five-parameter formula fits male full-time year-round workers, 1999. When we compare the fitting statistics with the Dagum in table 5.5, we see that the Dagum fits a little better if the CHISQ criterion is used, but the Champernowne fits a little better if any of the other three criteria are used. One must be cautioned not to assume that the Champernowne will always give a better fit on these criteria. Another sample survey may show better fits for the Dagum on all four criteria.

Cumulative Distribution Function

The CDF of the Champernowne five-parameter formula is defined over a slightly different domain than the other CDFs. That is $F(y)$ represents the

Table 5.6 Male Full-Time Year-Round Workers, 1999 (Numbers in Thousands of People): Computation of MAD, MSE, CHISQ, and K-S for the Champernowne Five-Parameter Formula: $\theta = .4395 \times 10^{-10}$, $\alpha = 2.6798$, $y_0 = 40{,}310$, $\sigma = .87859$

	Observed	Estimated	Pc. Diff.
Income Class ($)	f_0	f_c	% error
1–5,000	698	446	−36.1
5,000–10,000	1,009	1,770	75.4
10,000–15,000	3,217	3,226	0.3
15,000–25,000	9,944	9,569	−3.8
25,000–35,000	10,712	10,563	−1.4
35,000–50,000	12,457	12,601	1.2
50,000–75,000	10,914	10,777	−1.3
75,000+	8,569	8,568	−0.0
Total	57,520	57,520	
MAD = 228.5, MSE = 105,630, CHISQ = 490, K-S = .0090			

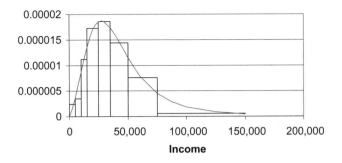

Figure 5.4. Male Full-Time Year-Round Workers, 1999: Champernowne Five-Parameter Formula, $\theta = .4395 \times 10^{-10}$, $\alpha = 2.6798$, $y_0 = 40{,}310$, $\sigma = .87859$

probable *number* of sampling units having an income above income level y. The conventional CDF is the probability of having an income below income level y. The formula is given as:

$$F(y) = \frac{N}{(1+\sigma)\theta}\left[(\sigma-1)\theta + 2\tan^{-1}\left\{\frac{\sin\theta}{\cos\theta + (y/y_0)^{\alpha\sigma}}\right\}\right], \leftrightarrow y < y_0$$

$$F(y) = \frac{2N\sigma}{(1+\sigma)\theta}\tan^{-1}\left\{\frac{\sin\theta}{\cos\theta + (y/y_0)^{\alpha}}\right\}, \leftrightarrow y \geq y_0.$$

From the CDF we note that the proportion of the sample above any income level y may be written as:

$$P = F(y)/N.$$

Substituting the five-parameter CDF and solving for y yields:

$$y = y_0\left\{\frac{\sin\theta}{\tan\left[\frac{\theta}{2}(p(1+\sigma) - \sigma + 1)\right]} - \cos\theta\right\}^{\frac{1}{\alpha\sigma}}, \leftrightarrow y \leq y_0$$

$$y = y_0\left\{\frac{\sin\theta}{\tan\left[\frac{\theta}{2\sigma}(1+\sigma)p\right]} - \cos\theta\right\}^{\frac{1}{\alpha}}, \leftrightarrow y > y_0.$$

Problems

1. Consider table 5.7 for females who work full-time and year-round in 1999.
   a. Compute the parameters of a log-logistic distribution for table 5.7.
   b. Compute the MAD, MSE, CHISQ, and K-S statistics for the fit in (a) above.
   c. Compare the fit in (b) above with the lognormal fit of problem 3.1 in chapter 3.

Table 5.7 Female Full-Time Year-Round Workers, 1999 (Numbers in Thousands of People)

Income Class Interval ($)	Number f_O
1–5,000	633
5,000–10,000	1,391
10,000–15,000	4,059
15,000–25,000	11,049
25,000–35,000	9,433
35,000–50,000	7,656
50,000–75,000	4,185
75,000+	2,015
Total	40,421
Mean income $33,303	

Source: U.S. Census Bureau, Money Income in the United States: 1999 (P60–209), Washington, GPO, 2000.

    d. Compute the probability that a randomly selected woman who is a full-time year-round worker will have an annual income above $80,000 and an annual income between $60,000 and $80,000. What is the income for women in this category at the 95th percentile?

2. Show that the parameter m is the logarithm of the median income for the log-logistic model.

3. Repeat problem 1 for the Singh-Maddala.

4. Differentiate the Singh-Maddala cumulative distribution function to obtain the income density function.

5. Repeat problem 1 for the Dagum.

Table 5.8 All U.S. Households by Total Money Income, 1999

Income Class ($)	Frequency Observed
.0001–5,000	3,010
5,000–10,000	6,646
10,000–15,000	7,660
15,000–25,000	14,720
25,000–35,000	13,271
35,000–50,000	16,539
50,000–75,000	19,272
75,000–100,000	10,755
100+	12,831

Source: U.S. Census Bureau, Money Income in the United States: 1999 (P60–209), Washington, GPO, 2000.

6. Estimate both the Dagum and Champernowne models for table 5.8 Leave the endpoints of the income classes in thousands of dollars. Compare the fit statistics between the two distributions.

References

1. Bartels, C. P. A. and H. van Metelen, *Alternative Probability Density Functions of Income*, Research Memorandum No. 29, Vrije University, Amsterdam, 1975, pp. 1–30.
2. Campano, F., *A Fresh Look at Champernowne's Five-Parameter Formula*, Economie appliquée, Vol. 40, 1987, pp. 162–175.
3. Champernowne, D. G., *The Graduation of Income Distributions*, Econometrica, No. 4, October 1952, pp. 591–615.
4. Dagum, C., *A Model of Income Distribution and the Conditions of Existence of Moments of Finite Order*, Proceeding of the 40th session of the International Statistical Institute, Vol. 46, Book 3, Warsaw, 1975, pp. 196–202.
5. Dagum, C., *A New Model of Personal Income Distribution: Specification and Estimation*, Economie appliquée, Vol. 30, 1977, pp. 413–437.
6. Fisk, P. R., *The Graduation of Income Distributions*, Econometrica, Vol. 29, 1961, pp. 171–185.
7. Gibrat, R., *Les Inégalités économiques*, Paris, Sirey, 1931, pp. 1–296.
8. Kloek, T. and H. K. Van Dijk, *Efficient Estimation of Income Distribution Parameters*, Journal of Econometrics, Vol. 8, 1978, pp. 61–74.
9. Pareto,V., *Cours d'économique politique*, Rouge, Lausanne, 1897, pp. 1–426.
10. Salem, A. B. Z. and T. D. Mount, *A Convenient Descriptive Model of Income Distribution*, Econometrica, Vol. 42, 1974, pp. 1115–1127.
11. Singh, S. K. and G. S. Maddala, *A Function for the Size Distribution of Incomes*, Econometrica, Vol. 44, 1976, pp. 481–486.
12. Suruga, T., *Functional Forms of Income Distribution: The Case of Yearly Income Groups in the "Annual Report on the Family Income and Expenditure Survey,"* Economic Studies Quarterly—Journal of the Japan Association of Economics and Econometrics, April 1982, pp. 361–395.
13. Thurow, L. *Analysing the American Income Distribution*, American Economic Review, Vol. 48, 1970, pp. 261–269.

6

Income Distribution
Summary Measures

An important advantage of modeling income distribution with continuous income density functions is that all summary statistics are derived from the estimated model. An alternative approach would be to estimate each statistic independently using discrete methods. The latter choice can, and often does, lead to measures that are not fully consistent with one another.

In this chapter we will demonstrate how a set of standard summary measures of income distribution can easily be estimated from the chosen model. There is of course an underlying assumption that the chosen model is the best-fitting model of the survey data. Among the more common income distribution summary measures that we will learn to estimate in this chapter are the measures of central tendency, namely, the mean, median, and mode; quantiles such as percentiles, deciles, and quintiles; and the Gini coefficient. The normative aspects of the Gini coefficient will be taken up in chapter 7 on income inequality. In the development of the estimation of the Gini coefficient, we will also learn to draw Lorenz curves from the selected model.

6.1 Measures of Central Tendency

In symmetrical distributions such as the normal or student's t-distribution, the main measures of central tendency, the mean, median, and mode, all fall in the same place, and hence it suffices to estimate only one of them as a measure of central tendency. The easiest choice is the mean or average because it only requires taking a sample of observations, adding them up, and dividing by the number of observations minus one. However, since income distributions are not symmetrical and skewed to the right, the mean, median, and mode are different.

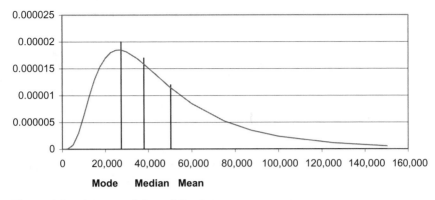

Figure 6.1. Measures of Central Tendency

In income distributions, the mode is lower than the median, which in turn is lower than the mean (figure 6.1). The more skewed the distribution, the greater the distance between them.

The mode is the measure that shows the highest concentration of incomes and is at the peak of the income density function. Modal incomes are useful in comparing income distributions of different groups. The median is the halfway point; that is, half of the population has an income more than the median and half less. This measure of central tendency is usually presented with the income survey but is more meaningful if it is presented with a set of quantiles such as deciles or quintiles. The mean income is probably the least useful of the three measures of central tendency because it is sensitive to the pull from a few income recipients with extraordinarily high incomes.

Estimating the Mean of the Distribution

For any continuous income density model we can obtain the mean directly from its definition using numerical integration:

$$\mu_y = E(y) = \int_{-\infty}^{\infty} yf(y)dy.$$

In the case of the lognormal distribution, it is not necessary to integrate because we can get the mean directly from the estimated parameters:

$$\mu_y = e^{\mu + \frac{\sigma^2}{2}}.$$

The lognormal estimates of μ and σ for male full-time year-round workers, 1999 from Example 2 in chapter 3 were 10.61189093 and .6581933, respectively. Hence $\mu_y = \$50,438$. However, for the log-logistic, Singh-Maddala, Dagum, and Champernowne distributions, numerical integration was used to obtain the mean. The results are shown in table 6.1.

Table 6.1 Male Full-Time Year-Round Workers, 1999: Comparison of Model Means with the Sample Mean (Sample Mean = $50,438)

Model	Mean	% Difference
Log-logistic	50,365	−0.14
Singh-Maddala	47,796	−5.24
Dagum	48,920	−3.01
Champernowne	48,612	−3.62

We notice that all of our models estimate the mean lower than the sample survey mean. There could be a number of explanations for this, but the most probable is that the sample contained a few males with exceptionally high incomes (these are called outliers), which pulled the sample mean to the right. This illustrates one of the difficulties in using the mean as a measure of central tendency in income distributions; namely, it can be influenced by a relatively small percentage of the high income population.

Estimating the Median of the Distribution

To estimate the median of the distribution, we will employ the inverse of the cumulative distribution function:

$$y = F^{-1}(.5).$$

Since we do not have an explicit CDF for the lognormal distribution, we cannot use this method for that distribution, but we do have inverse CDFs for the other four distributions. The median estimates for each is given in table 6.2. As we can see from table 6.2, the model and sample medians are much closer than the means in table 6.1. This is the general case, and it is one of the reasons that the median is a better measure of central tendency than the mean.

Estimating the Mode of the Distribution

The mode of the distribution is readily obtained by finding the maximum value of the income density function. This is a routine numerical technique and works well with even the most complicated functions. However, for the

Table 6.2 Male Full-Time Year-Round Workers, 1999: Comparison of Model Medians with the Sample Median (Sample Median = $37,574)

Model	Median	% Difference
Log-logistic	37,935	0.96
Singh-Maddala	38,418	2.24
Dagum	38,282	1.88
Champernowne	38,304	1.94

Table 6.3 Male Full-Time Year-Round Workers, 1999

Model	Parameters	Mode
Lognormal	$\mu = 10.61189093$, $\sigma = .6581933$	26,336
Log-logistic	$m = 10.544$, $k = .40363$	26,864
Singh-Maddala	$a_1 = .29112 \times 10^{-10}$, $a_2 = 2.2541$, $a_3 = 1.422$	27,606
Dagum	$\alpha = .35946 \times 10^{-06}$, $\beta = .83441$, $\lambda = 23,008$, $\delta = 2.685$	28,081
Champernowne*	$\theta = .4395 \times 10^{-10}$, $\alpha = 2.6798$, $y_0 = 40,310$, $\sigma = .87859$	27,399

*Numerical techniques were used to find max f(y) for the Champernowne.

lognormal, log-logistic, Singh-Maddala, and Dagum models the derivative yields an explicit solution for the mode of the distribution. These are given as follows:

$$\text{lognormal: } y_{\text{mode}} = e^{\mu - \sigma^2}$$

$$\text{log-logistic: } y_{\text{mode}} = \exp\left[m + k\ln\left(\frac{1-k}{1+k}\right)\right]$$

$$\text{Singh-Maddala: } y_{\text{mode}} = \exp\left[\frac{\ln\left(\frac{a_2-1}{a_1 a_2 a_3 + a_1}\right)}{a_2}\right]$$

$$\text{Dagum: } y_{\text{mode}} = \lambda^{\frac{1}{\delta}}\left(\frac{\beta\delta - 1}{\delta + 1}\right)^{\frac{1}{\delta}}, \ \beta\delta > 1.$$

The above formulas give the mean for male full-time year-round workers in table 6.3. Because the highest concentration of population has income around the mode, economic policies designed to affect the incomes around the mode will impact more population than policies that are focused on the mean or median. The distance (difference) between the mean and the mode is sometimes used as a measure of skewness of the income distribution.

6.2 Quantiles of Population Distributions

Reclassifying Income Classes

Quite often, the researcher will want a different set of income classes than the one given in the summary table of the income distribution survey. For example, one might be interested in income classes of deciles or quintiles of the population. Such a reclassification is quite easy if the income distribution model has a CDF that can be inverted algebraically. For example, suppose it is decided to have the population divided into deciles by income classes—that is, ten groups with the same population size but sorted by income. We then set $p_1 = .1$, $p_2 = .2$, $p_3 = .3, \ldots, p_9 = .9$ and plug them into the CDF inverse, and we will obtain the income cutoffs for the ten groups.

Table 6.4 Male Full-Time Year-Round Workers, 1999:
Decile Income Brackets

Income Class ($)	Percent of Population
0–15,444	10
15,445–21,775	10
21,776–27,211	10
27,212–32,549	10
32,550–38,259	10
38,260–44,862	10
44,863–53,236	10
53,237–65,427	10
65,428–88,905	10
88,905 +	10

In the case of the Dagum estimate of the male full-time year-round workers, 1999, the inverse of the CDF is given by:

$$y = 23,008^{\frac{1}{2.685}} \left[\left(\frac{1 - .35946 \times 10^{-6}}{p - .35946 \times 10^{-6}} \right)^{\frac{1}{.83441}} - 1 \right]^{\frac{-1}{2.685}}.$$

Substituting $p_1 = .1$, $p_2 = .2$, $p_3 = .3, \ldots, p_9 = .9$, we get the reclassified income distribution shown in table 6.4. This table does not show the share of income that each decile receives. However, we can estimate the flow of income to each decile by integrating over the first moment function $g(y) = yf(y)$. That is:

$$\int_{y_1}^{y_2} g(y)dy = \text{the amount of income flowing to the bracket}$$

bounded by y_1 and y_2 divided by the total population. Hence the amount of income flowing to the bracket is:

$$N \int_{y_1}^{y_2} g(y)dy,$$

where N is the total population.

To see why the above is true, note that for a continuous function $g(y)$ and a partition of the income axis by 0, $y_1, y_2, \ldots, y_n$, the following is true:

$$\frac{Y}{N} = \mu_y = E(y)$$

$$= \int_0^\infty g(y)dy$$

$$= \int_0^{y_1} g(y)dy + \int_{y_1}^{y_2} g(y)dy + \int_{y_2}^{y_3} g(y)dy + \cdots + \int_{y_n}^\infty g(y)dy,$$

where Y is the total income for the society—hence for the income brackets that define the deciles, the income flows (obtained by numerical integration, which may be done with standard mathematical software on a PC or a calculator that has numerical integration functions).

For the Dagum fit of male full-time year-round workers, $g(y)$ is given by:

$$g(y) = \frac{(1-\alpha)\lambda\beta\delta}{y^\delta(1+\lambda y^{-\delta})^{\beta+1}}$$
$$= \frac{(1-.35946\times 10^{-06})(23{,}008)(.83441)(2.685)}{y^{2.685}(1+23{,}008y^{-2.685})^{1.83441}}.$$

The amount of income flowing to the second decile that is bounded by y_1 and y_2 can be computed using numerical integration of:

$$57{,}520 \int_{15{,}445}^{21{,}775} \frac{51{,}546.91268}{y^{2.685}(1+23{,}008y^{-2.685})^{1.83441}}\, dy = 107{,}812.$$

To get the second decile's share of income, divide the amount of income computed in the above integral by the total income, which is $N\mu_y = 57{,}520(48{,}911) = 2{,}813{,}361$, and show the percentage.

The results for all deciles are shown in table 6.5.

6.3 The Lorenz Curve and Gini Coefficient

The Lorenz Curve

The Lorenz curve is a graph showing the relationship between the cumulative population as arranged from poorest to richest and their corresponding cumulative income. The decile distribution in table 6.5 produces the Lorenz curve in figure 6.2.

The horizontal axis in figure 6.2 shows the cumulative population and the vertical axis the corresponding cumulative income. The diagonal represents an

Table 6.5 Male Full-Time Year-Round Workers, 1999:
Income and Income Shares by Decile

Decile	Income ($\times 1{,}000$)	Income Share
1	60,739	2.16
2	107,812	3.83
3	141,062	5.01
4	171,797	6.11
5	203,355	7.23
6	238,466	8.48
7	280,959	9.99
8	338,556	12.03
9	434,134	15.43
10	836,481	29.73
Total Income	2,813,361	

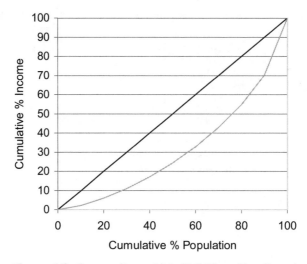

Figure 6.2. Lorenz Curve Male Full-Time Year-Round
Workers, 1999

income distribution where all income recipients have exactly the same income.
That is, the first decile will have 10% of the total income; the first and second
deciles will have together 20% of the total income; the first, second, and third
deciles will have together 30% of the total income; and so on. The curved line
below the diagonal is the Lorenz curve for male full-time year-round workers.
It shows that the first decile only has 2.16% of the total income; the first and
second deciles together have 5.99% of the total income (2.16% and 3.83%);
the first, second, and third together have 11% of the total income (5.99% and
5.01%); and so on.

The more *unequal* the distribution of income, the greater the separation
between the diagonal and the Lorenz curve. Hence, the Lorenz curve is a
visual way of assessing the inequality of income in a population group. In the
extreme case, where one income recipient had all the income (therefore, all
others had none), the Lorenz curve would be formed by the horizontal axis and
the right side of the figure. In comparing the Lorenz curves of two groups, it is
generally possible to state which group has the greater inherent inequality by
comparing the separation of the Lorenz curves from the diagonal as long as the
Lorenz curves do not intersect. If the Lorenz curve intersect, then no comparison can be made about the inequality inherent in the groups. These cases
are illustrated in figures 6.3 and 6.4, respectively.

The Gini Coefficient

While the Lorenz curve gives a visual sense of the degree of inequality of
income distribution, the Gini coefficient gives a measurable index of inequality.

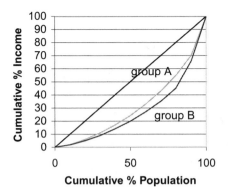

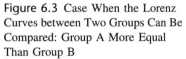

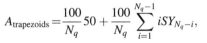

Figure 6.3 Case When the Lorenz Curves between Two Groups Can Be Compared: Group A More Equal Than Group B

Probably the most widely used measure of income inequality, the Gini coefficient is the ratio of the area between the diagonal and the Lorenz curve and the area of the triangle below the diagonal. It is easy to see that if a society has a perfectly equitable income distribution—that is, the Lorenz curve coincides with the diagonal—that ratio would be 0. On the other hand, if the other extreme were the case—that is, all income is concentrated in one income recipient—then the Lorenz curve would consist of the two legs of the triangle below the diagonal, and the Gini coefficient would be 1. Hence, the Gini coefficient lies between 0 and 1. The closer to 0 the Gini is, the more equally distributed the income.

We can estimate the Gini coefficient for a quantile distribution by adding up the areas of the trapezoids that lie below the Lorenz curve and subtracting the total from 5,000, which is the area of the triangle. This yields the area between the diagonal and the Lorenz curve. The next step is to divide this area by 5,000. The formula for finding the sum of the trapezoid areas is given by:

$$A_{\text{trapezoids}} = \frac{100}{N_q} 50 + \frac{100}{N_q} \sum_{i=1}^{N_q-1} iSY_{N_q-i},$$

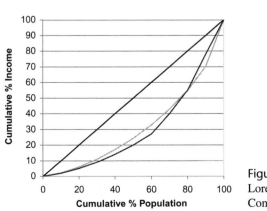

Figure 6.4. Case Where the Lorenz Curves Cannot Be Compared

Table 6.6 Male Full-Time Year-Round Workers, 1999: Gini Coefficient Computations: Income and Income Shares by Decile

Decile	SY	$iSY_{Nq\text{-}1}$
1	2.16	$1 \times 15.43 = 15.43$
2	3.83	$2 \times 12.03 = 24.06$
3	5.01	$3 \times 9.99 = 29.97$
4	6.11	$4 \times 8.48 = 33.92$
5	7.23	$5 \times 7.23 = 36.15$
6	8.48	$6 \times 6.11 = 36.66$
7	9.99	$7 \times 5.01 = 35.07$
8	12.03	$8 \times 3.83 = 30.64$
9	15.43	$9 \times 2.16 = 19.44$
10	29.73	
Total	100.00	261.34

Area under Lorenz curve $= 10 \times 50 + 10 \times 261.34 = 3{,}113.4$.
Area between Diagonal and Lorenz curve $= 5{,}000 - 3{,}113.4 = 1{,}886.6$, Gini coefficient $= 1{,}886.6/5{,}000 = .37732$.

where $N_q =$ the number of quantiles—that is, 5 for quintiles, 10 for deciles, and 100 for percentiles—and SY_q is the share of income in percent flowing to the q quantile.

Table 6.6 shows the computations for finding the Gini coefficient for male full-time year-round workers in 1999 in terms of deciles. Figure 6.5 shows the corresponding Lorenz curve.

It should be noted that the above estimate of the Gini coefficient could be improved if percentiles were used instead of deciles. In that case, the Gini coefficient would have been slightly higher at .3804. Furthermore, it is possible to obtain a more precise estimate of the Gini coefficient using a model and numerical integration:

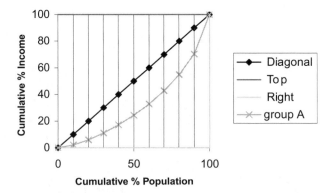

Figure 6.5. Gini Coefficient for Male Full-Time Year-Round Workers, 1999

$$\text{Gini} = \frac{2}{\mu_y} \int_0^\infty g(y)F(y)dy - 1,$$

where $g(y)$ is the first moment function and $F(y)$ is the CDF. For the example of male full-time year-round workers and the Dagum distribution, this is reduced to:

$$\text{Gini} = \frac{2}{\mu_y} \int_0^\infty \frac{(1-\alpha)\lambda\beta\delta}{y^\delta(1+\lambda\cdot y^{-\delta})^{\beta+1}} \left[\alpha + \frac{1-\alpha}{(1+\lambda\cdot y^{-\delta})^\beta} \right] dy - 1.$$

Substituting the estimated parameters yields:

$$\text{Gini} = \frac{2}{48.911} \int_0^\infty \frac{51{,}546.91268}{y^{2.685}(1+23{,}008y^{-2.685})^{1.83441}}$$
$$\times \left[\frac{1}{(1+23{,}008y^{-2.685})^{.83441}} \right] dy - 1.$$

This can be simplified to:

$$\text{Gini} = \frac{2}{48.911} \int_0^\infty \frac{51{,}546.91268}{y^{2.685}(1 + 23{,}008y^{-2.685})^{2.66882}} dy - 1 = .3872.$$

Problems

1. Using the data for female full-time year-round workers, 1999 (see problem 1, chapter 3), compute the mean based upon the log-logistic, Singh-Maddala, Dagum, and Champernowne distributions.
2. Repeat problem 1 for the mode and median.
3. Use the Dagum distribution to find the decile distribution for female full-time year-round workers, 1999.
4. Based on the decile distribution found in problem 3, draw the Lorenz curve and estimate the Gini coefficient.

Reference

Kakwani, Nanak C., *Income Inequality and Poverty*, A World Bank Research Publication, New York, Oxford University Press, 1980.

Supplement to Chapter 6

Using a Spreadsheet to Graph the Lorenz Curve

Figure 6.2 was drawn using *EXCEL*. The data in the spreadsheet are presented in table 6.7. The first column, which is labeled population, is the horizontal axis of the graph. The second column yields the diagonal, the third column

Table 6.7 Spreadsheet Data for the Lorenz Curve

Population	Diagonal	Top	Right	Cum Shares
0	0	100	0	0
10	10	100	0	2.16
20	20	100	0	5.99
30	30	100	0	11
40	40	100	0	17.11
50	50	100	0	24.34
60	60	100	0	32.82
70	70	100	0	42.81
80	80	100	0	54.84
90	90	100	0	70.27
100	100	100	0	100
100	100	100	100	100

draws the top border, and the fourth column draws the right-side border. The Lorenz curve is based on the last column, which is the cumulative shares of income from the decile distribution. Note that the last row is necessary to position the pen for the right-side border.

Numerical Integration

It is quite easy to do numerical integration these days. It shows up on discounted mathematical software sold in bookstores, it is somewhere in every college and university in their computer software libraries, and it can even be found on some hand-held graphic calculators. However, some students prefer to have their own software in their personal computers. The program listed below is written in BASIC and can be installed on any computer that supports BASIC.

```
REM PROGRAM TO ESTIMATE THE AMOUNT OF INCOME
FLOWING TO THE INCOME
REM BRACKET BOUNDED BY Y1 AND Y2 USING THE DAGUM
MODEL
INPUT " ENTER THE LOWER INCOME OF THE BRACKET " ; Y1
INPUT " ENTER THE UPPER INCOME OF THE BRACKET " ; Y2
A = Y1
B = Y2
REM SET THE PARAMETERS OF THE DAGUM DISTRIBUTION
REM THESE PERTAIN TO THE ESTIMATES OF MALE FULL-
TIME YEAR-ROUND
REM WORKERS 1999 AND MUST BE CHANGED FOR ANOTHER
SURVEY
```

```
REM FIRST SET ALPHA
Alf = .35946 * 10 ^ -6
REM NEXT SET BETA
BET = .83441
REM NEXT SET LAMBDA
LAM = 23008
REM FINALLY DELTA
DEL = 2.685
REM ALSO SET THE TOTAL SAMPLE SIZE
TP = 57520
NN=1000
GOSUB 100
AMT FLO*TP
PRINT " THE AMOUNT OF INCOME FLOWING TO THE INCOME
BRACKET "
PRINT " BOUNDED BY " ; Y1; " AND " ; Y2; " IS " ; AMT
PRINT " "
END
100 REM NUMERICAL INTEGRATION FOR THE AMOUNT OF
    INCOME FLOWING
    REM TO THE INCOME BRACKET BOUNDED BY A AND B
      TWOH = (B - A) / NN
      H = TWO / 2
      SUMEND = 0
      SUMMID = 0
      FOR K = 1 TO NN
            XK1 = K - 1
            X = A + (XK1 * TWOH)
            XX = X
            GOSUB 200
            SUMEND = SUMEND + G
            XX = X + H
            GOSUB 200
            SUMMID = SUMMID + G
      NEXT K
      XX = A
      GOSUB 200
      GA = G
      XX = B
      GOSUB 200
      GB = G
      FLO = (2 * SUMEND + 4 * SUMMID - GA + GB) * H/3
RETURN
```

```
200 REM FIRST MOMENT FUNCTION FOR THE DAGUM
      YYY = CDBL(YYY)
      XXX = CDBL(XXX)
      IF XX <= 0 THEN GOTO 210
      XXX = (1 - ALF) * BET * LAM * DEL / (XX ^ DEL)
      YYY = 1 + (LAM / (XX ^ DEL))
      ZZZ = BET + 1
      LNG = LOG(XXX) - ZZZ * LOG(YYY)
      G = EXP(LNG)
    210 REM
RETURN
```

7

Income Inequality

In a resolution adopted by the Twelfth Central Committee of the Chinese Communist Party (September 28, 1986) on the guiding principles for building a socialist society with advanced culture and society, a few surprising points were made. One was: "It is wrong to regard Marxism as a rigid dogma. It is also wrong to negate its basic tenets, view it as an outmoded theory and blindly worship bourgeois philosophies and social doctrines." This was a surprise because it was assumed by most people outside of China that Marxism was rigid and could not be compromised. And related to this point was that the effort to encourage scientific debate on democratic policy making required "letting a hundred flowers bloom, a hundred schools of thought contend." Party officials were told to "take economic development as the key link," and while "Socialist ethics means love of the motherland, the people, labor, science, socialism," nevertheless, "we shall on no account regard egalitarianism as an ethical principle in our society" (*China Daily*, Vol. 6, No. 1616, Monday, September 29, 1986). In this regard, it left in place a government policy allowing some Chinese to get rich more quickly than others.

There is probably no other area of economics that is more dependent on normative economics than inequality. If China cannot support a policy of equality of income, what country can? On the other hand, how much inequality can be tolerated? Certainly, no country could stay together if one income recipient had all the income. Should there be a limit on the salaries of chief executive officers of major corporations? How do we measure inequality? Is there an ideal measure? These are just a few of the many unanswered questions that arise in the study of inequality. In this chapter you will get an introduction to the study of inequality, starting with reasons why inequality may naturally happen in a market society.

7.1 Income Inequality within Countries

Income Distribution Surveys Revisited

As mentioned in chapter 2, the household is the choice of income recipient in the sample surveys of most countries. The United States, which has one of the most advanced statistical offices (U.S. Census Bureau), collects data on families and individuals as well, but this is the exception rather than the rule. In most developing countries, if any survey exists at all, it will be based on households as income recipients. An important difference between a family and a household as the income recipient is that families must have two or more people living together, whereas a household may contain only one person. However, since households are more commonly used as income recipients, we will begin our study of income inequality by comparing the income differences between households.

In a survey, an interviewer will find that for any two randomly selected households either the income will be the same or different. If every household in the survey has the same income, the Gini coefficient will be 0. The other extreme would be that only one household has income (all the rest have none), in which case the Gini will be 1. Clearly, the first alternative is better than the second. In general, the lower the Gini coefficient, the more evenly the income is distributed among households, and the more positive is the image of the society from a social justice point of view. This is of course a normative statement, but it is a view probably shared by most people.

It should be noted here that comparisons of Gini coefficients can be tricky; for example, if Lorenz curves cross, then it is not clear that the lower Gini coefficient is indicative of the more even distribution of income. Some people argue that a high Gini coefficient, providing it is not extremely high, say, above .6, is not in itself a matter of concern as long as there is income mobility in the society. That is, if it is possible for people to move from low incomes to high incomes in their lifetimes because they are highly motivated and make the right decisions about career choices, then there will be income mobility in the society. This view is also normative and is probably shared by a minority of people.

Gini computations are affected by the definition of income. When taxes and cash income transfers are taken into account, the Gini coefficient tends to lower. This can be seen for the United States in table 7.1. Ideally, all countries should compute the Gini coefficient after taxes and cash transfers, but most countries do not have that information. In the case of the United States, a progressive tax structure and cash transfers to the poorer populations act to redistribute a fraction of the income.

There are several reasons why one household may have a significantly higher income than another, and some of these reasons have general social

Table 7.1 United States 1992 and 1998: Household Gini
Coefficient by Definition of Income

Definition of Income	1992	1998
Definition 1 (Official Measure)	.430	.446
Definition 4 (definition 1 less government cash transfers plus capital gains and employee health benefits)	.497	.509
Definition 8 (definition 4 less taxes, includes EIC)	.471	.484
Definition 11 (definition 8 plus non-means-tested government cash transfers)	.404	.419
Definition 14 (definition 11 plus means-tested government cash transfers)	.385	.405
Definition 15 (definition 14 plus return on home equity)	.381	.399

Sources: U.S. Census Bureau, *Money Income in the United States: 1992*, Washington, GPO, 1993; U.S. Census Bureau, *Money Income in the United States: 1998* (P60–206), Washington, GPO, 1999.

acceptance. In some cases, the differences may be attributed to discrimination; that is, they may be based on race or gender. These situations are illegal in the United States, but enforcement of the law can be difficult, especially in small firms. In some countries, the discrimination is blatant, with no laws protecting minorities or women.

Reasons Why Household Income Might Differ

a. *The number of wage earners in the household.* Differences in income can occur between two households of similar characteristics if the number of wage earners is different. For example, in the United States during 1998 Asian and Pacific Islanders had the highest median household income among racial groups ($46,637), followed by non-Hispanic white households ($42,439). However, the average size of the Asian and Pacific Islander household was 3.15, as compared with 2.47 for non-Hispanic white households. The larger-sized household has more potential wage earners, especially if there are older children living at home who are finished with school. Consider also the case of an engaged couple living separately in two single-person households. If they both have the same income, they will double their household income after they are married and move into the same household.

b. *Educational attainment of the wage earners in the household.* Table 7.2 shows the average earnings by level of education and by gender, in which there is a strong correlation between educational level and wage earnings. The microeconomic explanation for this is that the more education a person has, the more opportunity he or she has to produce expensive products, thereby yielding a higher marginal revenue product

Table 7.2 U.S. Full-Time Year-Round Workers, 1999:
Median Income by Educational Attainment

Educational Attainment	Male	Female
Less Than 9th Grade	$20,429	$15,098
9th to 12th Grade (No Degree)	25,035	17,015
High School Graduate	33,184	23,061
Some College (No Degree)	39,221	27,757
Associate Degree	41,638	30,919
Bachelor's Degree	52,985	37,993
Master's Degree	66,243	48,097
Doctorate Degree	81,687	60,079
Professional Degree (i.e., J.D., M.D., M.B.A.)	100,000	59,904

Source: U.S. Census Bureau, *Money Income in the United States: 1999* (P60–209), Washington, GPO, 2000, table 7.

than people with less education. Employers are willing to pay higher wages for a higher marginal revenue product. Furthermore, on the supply side of the labor market, the attraction of higher wages for higher levels of education provides an incentive for continuing education. As the proportion of the population that seeks higher education increases, society in general benefits because better-educated citizens are more productive and socially more responsible.

c. *Location of employment of the wage earners in the household.* Where one is employed can make a large difference in the wages that are earned. Many people commute long distances because of higher earning potential in another location. There are regional differences in the United States. The median household income (based on a 3-year average from 1997 to 1999) in the United States varied from a low of $28,398 in Arkansas to a high of $51,046 in Alaska. Among the lower 48 states, Maryland had the highest median household income at $50,630, followed by New Jersey at $50,234. The median household income for the United States as a whole was $39,657. However, in interpreting these data one must take into account the cost of living in the various states. The real (inflation-adjusted) income has a lower variance. Nevertheless, these differences are reflected in the Gini coefficient for the country as a whole.

d. *Age of the wage earners in the household.* In table 7.3 we see that younger and older members of the labor force tend to have lower incomes than middle-aged people. In 1999, householders who were between 45 and 54 years old had the highest median household income, at $56,917.

From the microeconomic point of view, wages should vary with age if productivity also varies with age. One would expect that as people grow older,

Table 7.3 U.S. Median Household Income by Age of
Householder, 1989, 1998, 1999 (in Real 1999 $)

Age (years)	1989	1998	1999
15–24	$24,940	$24,084	$25,171
25–34	39,903	40,954	42,174
35–44	50,399	49,521	50,873
45–54	55,780	55,344	56,917
55–64	41,465	44,120	44,597
65+	21,177	22,209	22,812

Source: U.S. Census Bureau, *Money Income in the United States: 1999*
(P60–209), Washington, GPO, 2000.

experience will teach them to do their job more efficiently. The increased productivity leads to higher marginal revenue product and hence a willingness of firms to pay higher wages. Most wage earners expect increases in wages from time to time. Often, people will change jobs if they think that their employer is too slow in awarding wage increases.

From a social justice point of view, it makes some sense that younger and older aged households have less income than middle-aged households. Households with children have a greater need for income when the principal wage earners are middle age than at any other time. This is because their children are teenagers about then, and dependent teenage children require much more of the household's resources than their younger siblings, especially if they go on to higher education.

At retirement age, the children have left the household, and the cost of housing itself is generally less because if the mortgage is not paid up by then, it usually is low compared to the mortgage that younger people pay who have not lived in their houses as long. Likewise, if the older person is renting, there is a good chance that the rent is low because the older person has been in the apartment for a long time. Furthermore, older people have the option to move to communities that have a lower cost of living because they are not constrained to a location for employment purposes. Hence, most people will agree that older people do not (aside for medical expenses, which in the United States are subsidized by Medicare) have as great a need for income as middle-aged families raising children.

Paglin's Basic Revision of the Gini Coefficient

In a much cited paper appearing in the September 1975 issue of the *American Economic Review*, Morton Paglin [13] argued for an alternative to the conventional Gini coefficient (which he labels as the Lorenz-Gini). He advocated that, first, the income recipient should be families rather than households. The main reason is that households may contain only one person, and he estimated that this alone can make a 29% difference in the computation of the Gini. He

Table 7.4 Total Income of Families by Age of Householder, 1999

Age (years)	Number of Families	Mean Income ($)	Total Income ($)
15–24	3,353	29,939	100,385,467
25–34	13,009	52,562	683,779,058
35–44	18,708	66,996	1,253,361,168
45–54	15,804	79,897	1,262,692,188
55–64	9,569	70,582	675,399,158
65–74	7,025	50,110	352,022,750
75+	4,562	40,347	184,063,014

Source: U.S. Census Bureau, *Money Income in the United States: 1999* (P60–209), Washington, GPO, 2000, table A.

pointed out all the reasons for differences in household income mentioned above but was particularly concerned with the differences emanating out of the age of the family income earners.

He proposed that equality of family income should be defined in terms of *family lifetime income* but not equal incomes for all families at one point in time. Instead, every family at a given stage of its life cycle would have the same income, and all families would have equal lifetime incomes. Age-related family income needs vary, and it would be unrealistic to insist that each family have the same income. However, a reasonable goal would be that all families have the same lifetime income. His proposal was to correct the Lorenz-Gini by subtracting the natural variance in household income as measured in an age-related or *age-Gini*. The resulting number would be called the Paglin-Gini (or P-Gini). Hence, one could compute the Paglin-Gini by first computing the Gini in the usual fashion and then subtracting the age-Gini.

We will illustrate how to compute the age-Gini by going through the computations on *U.S. families in 1999*, shown in table 7.4. The first step is to take the data in table 7.4 and sort the age groups by mean income, then compute the percentage of families in each age group and their percentage of total income. Next, compute the cumulative percentages of families and income. These will form the base of the age-related inequality curve. The steps are shown in table 7.5.

The percentage of families and percentage of income in table 7.5 are computed by dividing the number of families and the total income into the sum of the number of families and the sum of total income, respectively. The last two columns are obtained by cumulating the percentages. Finally, a quadratic[1]

---

[1]Paglin used a cubic-spline function rather than a quadratic. We found that by using a simple quadratic we arrive at the same age-Gini coefficients, provided that our numerical integration technique used at least 3,000 trapezoids.

Table 7.5 Cumulative Income of Families by Age of Householder, 1999

Age (years)	No. of Fam.	Mean ($)	Total Income ($)	% Fam	% Y Cum	% Fam Cum	% Y
15–24	3,353	29,939	100,385,467	4.66	2.23	4.66	2.23
75+	4,562	40,347	184,063,014	6.33	4.08	10.99	6.31
65–74	7,025	50,110	352,022,750	9.75	7.80	20.75	14.11
25–34	13,009	52,562	683,779,058	18.06	15.16	38.81	29.27
35–44	18,708	66,996	1,253,361,168	25.97	27.78	64.78	57.05
55–64	9,569	70,582	675,399,158	13.28	14.97	78.06	72.02
45–54	15,804	79,897	1,262,692,188	21.94	27.99	100.00	100.00
Total	72,030		4,511,702,803				

Note: Y is a symbol for income.

regression function (constant term suppressed) was fitted to the last two columns to get a continuous curve from which to compute the age-Gini. The regression yielded the following function:

$$cum\%Y = 0.612152cum\%fam + .003927(cum\%fam)^2.$$

Using the software package *P-Gini*, a Gini coefficient was computed between the diagonal line and the above function to produce the age-Gini. The result is the age-Gini $= .1263$. The data in table 7.6 were used with the Dagum model to produce the Lorenz-Gini of .4255. Hence the Paglin-Gini is $.4255 - .1263 = .2992$.

Paglin's revision to the Lorenz-based Gini coefficient is appealing because the assumption of equal income for families with householder at the same age, and equal lifetime incomes for all families, seems to be more realistic than a concept of equal income for all families regardless of the age of the householder. It separates the issue of intrafamily variation in income over the life cycle from the more basic issue of interfamily differences in lifetime incomes.

Table 7.6 All Families Income Distribution, 1999

Income Bracket ($)	Number of Families (×1,000)
0–5,000	1,740
5,000–9,999	2,404
10,000–14,999	3,485
15,000–24,999	8,678
25,000–34,999	8,550
35,000–49,999	11,861
50,000–74,999	15,236
75,000–99,999	9,120
100,000+	10,956

Response to Paglin's Basic Revision

Five comments on Paglin's paper (as well as his reply) appeared in the June 1977 issue of the *American Economic Review*. The authors, while in agreement with Paglin's idea of correcting the Gini for differences in age of householder, found technical problems in his methodology.

Eric R. Nelson (University of Michigan) [12] argued that the mere subtracting of the age-Gini from the Lorenz-Gini does not produce the true Paglin-Gini, which isolates the issue of intrafamily income variation from that of interfamily differences. To see this, the Lorenz-Gini should be disaggregated into measures of intragroup concentration and between-group concentration. In the limiting case, where families are grouped by income magnitude so group distributions do not overlap, the between-group term is identical to Paglin's age-Gini. However, income distributions by cohort do overlap extensively, so Paglin's age-Gini underestimates the absolute age-income term, and it follows the P-Gini is overestimated.

In his reply, Paglin agrees that cohort income distributions overlap but the overlap produces an interaction term[2] that is related to the degree of within-cohort inequality. He argues that this is taken into account by his age-Gini, whereas it would be overlooked by Nelson's version of the age-Gini.

In his comment, William R. Johnson [8] of the University of Virginia uses a model to demonstrate that the Paglin-Gini will always underestimate the *true extent* of lifetime income inequality. Paglin replies by agreeing that the P-Gini does not indicate actual differences in lifetime incomes, but he reminds us that this was pointed out in his paper. On the other hand, he disagrees with the main conclusion that the P-Gini will always underestimate the true extent of lifetime income inequality. He argues that Johnson arrives at that conclusion because his model is too simple and does not allow for intracohort income mobility.

Sheldon Danziger, Robert Haveman, and Eugene Smolensky [4] of the Institute for Research on Poverty, University of Wisconsin, submitted a comment in which they found the P-Gini to give counterintuitive results when comparing the years 1965 with 1972. However, Paglin found an error in their method of computing the P-Gini and dismissed their criticism.

In another comment, Joseph L. Minarik [11], of the Brookings Institution, modified the P-Gini to incorporate education as well as age. While this lowered the absolute inequality in any one year, the trend of inequality over time was

---

[2]The analysis of the within-cohort interaction term is based upon a game matrix devised by Graham Pyatt [1976], whose cells represent expected gains of all individuals when placed in a game setting in which each draws the incomes of other persons at random but keeps his own income if the income drawn is of lower value. Since Pyatt used a variant of the discrete form of the Gini formula where the average of absolute income differences is replaced by the average expected gain, the Gini coefficient can be interpreted as the average expected gain as a percent of the mean income.

increasing rather than decreasing, as Paglin found. Paglin answered by arguing that it is a reasonable goal that families have equal lifetime incomes even if they have unequal incomes at different ages, but education-related differences in families do not tend to "wash out" in the long run. On the other hand, he added that the disaggregation of the Lorenz-Gini into the age-Gini component and a residual in the current year is meaningful because it can help policy makers identify the importance of their contribution to inequality.

The fifth comment in this series was presented by C. John Kurien [10] of McGill University. He suggested that "from a welfare point of view . . . the most useful partition is variation related to differences in opportunities among persons and its residual, choice-related variation." The ideal measure of income distribution would eliminate the latter. He argues that the Paglin-Gini eliminates only a part of the choice-related variation and also some of the opportunity-related variation, making it difficult to accept the "definiteness of his [Paglin's] conclusions." Paglin concedes that this proposal seems reasonable, but it cannot really be used in a measure because of the "complex interconnection between choices and opportunities." He uses the number of children that a family chooses to have as an example of choice-related variation and poses the policy question: "[S]hould we require small families to subsidize the choice-related decisions of the large families?" If the choice-related variation is eliminated, the measure will not be of much help in answering this kind of question.

Three other responses to Paglin's basic revision appeared later in the *American Economic Review*, one by Kenneth Wertz [17] in September 1979, another by John P. Formby and Terry G. Seaks [5] in June 1980, and a third by Formby, Seaks, and W. James Smith [6] in March 1989. Of these, the last paper is the one that seems to cast the most doubt on the interpretation of the age- and consequently the Paglin-Gini. In their earlier paper, Formby and Seaks embrace Paglin's revision but add a refinement called the MP-Gini, which varies between 0 and 1, as does the Lorenz-Gini. This is a desirable quality for an inequality measure, since 0 is associated with the ideal situation and 1 with the worst situation. However, in their 1989 paper with Smith, they demonstrate how the magnitude of the P-Gini can change with the age partition size.

Working with the microdata from the March *Current Population Survey* tapes for the years from 1967 to 1986, they computed the P-Gini for age partitions of one year, five years, ten years, and twenty years (Paglin's original paper used a 10-year partition except for the 65 and over class). Table 2 of Formby, Seaks, and Smith's paper shows how the P-Gini changes in magnitude for each of these age partitions. They further argue that by varying the width of the age groupings, they can ascribe any degree of inequality, from 0 to the entire amount. However, the year-to-year direction of change in inequality was consistent over the whole period for all age partitions but differed in level.

Paglin replied to this by arguing that the P-Gini should be computed from a large sample, and reducing the age partition reduces sample size for each partition and hence increases sampling error. If this is carried out to the extreme, where the age groups are based on a sample of one, they become as erratic as individual income and impose an upward bias on the age-Gini. However, conceptually, the age-Gini is refined by using smaller age partitions. The optimal partition occurs when a reduction in the age partition does not yield a significant change in the age-Gini. This can work for large sample surveys (i.e., 42,000 families or more) partitioned at 65 one-year intervals. One difficulty with this reply is that the measure now becomes dependent on very large sample surveys, which are not feasible in all countries.

7.2 Other Inequality Measures

While the Gini coefficient is the most commonly used measure of income inequality, several others have been proposed. We will look at a few of these that have at least some of the more desirable properties researchers look for in inequality measures.

The first desirable property is the range of the measure. If one wants to make a judgment about the extent of inequality, it is useful to have a measure that has a range between two numbers, one representing the most even distribution of income and another representing the case when one income recipient has all the income—that is, as in the case of the Gini, which varies between 0 and 1. A second desirable property is to have a measure that remains the same if all income recipients see the same percentage change in their incomes. Finally, the third desirable property is to have a measure that reflects transfers between the rich and the poor. One would expect that the measure shows more equality if a rich person transfers income to a poor person, and vice versa.[3] The choice of an inequality measure is often based on the above properties.

For mathematically advanced students, deeper insight into the decision of selecting an inequality measure is given in Champernowne [2], Champernowne and Cowell [3], Frosini [7], and Kakwani [9].

The Coefficient of Variation

One of the simplest measures of inequality is the coefficient of variation given by dividing the mean of the income distribution by the standard deviation. That is:

$$CV = \frac{\sigma_y}{\mu_y}.$$

The smaller the standard deviation, the more incomes will be clustered around the mean. In the case where all income recipients have the same income,

---

[3]Here we are assuming that the transfer does not change the ranking of the income recipients. This is called the Pigou-Dalton principle of transfers.

the standard deviation will be 0, and hence the coefficient of variation will also be 0. Although it is sensitive to transfers at all levels of income, the coefficient of variation does not have the desirable property of being bounded from above.

An Inequality Measure Suggested by Theil

Henri Theil [16] proposed the following inequality measure:

$$T = \ln(\mu_y) - \int_0^\infty \ln(y)f(y)dy.$$

The integral may be regarded as the natural logarithm of the geometric mean (μ_{gm}) of the distribution. Therefore, the measure may be more concisely written as:

$$T = \ln(\mu_y) - \ln(\mu_{gm}) = \ln\left(\frac{\mu_y}{\mu_{gm}}\right).$$

The geometric mean will always be less than the mean, except in the case when all elements of the population have exactly the same income. The density function in such a case would be an *atomic* distribution characterized by one point; that is, the probability of any income other than the mean income would be 0, and hence the geometric mean, median, and mode would all be equal. The measure would then be $T = n(1) = 0$. If, on the other hand, $T > 0$, then the income distribution is skewed to the right, and the greater T, the worse the skewness. Recall that extreme right-hand skewness occurs when a few income recipients have enormous incomes as compared to all the rest of the income recipients. The worst case is when one recipient has all the income.

Unfortunately, the *T* measure is not bounded above by 1, as is the Gini, so it is difficult to get a sense of how badly skewed the distribution is simply by looking at the number. On the other hand, the *T* measure addresses a very important socioeconomic question that is based on human characteristics. For large populations of humans, almost all human characteristics are *normally* distributed and hence symmetric distributions. Intelligence, physical size, work attitudes, dexterity, and so on, are all normally distributed. However, income distribution is skewed and hence asymmetric. This is counterintuitive; it would seem as though income should also be symmetrically distributed, reflecting the normality of human populations. It should also be mentioned that a more advanced treatment of the Theil measure would also indicate another useful feature of this statistic, that is, how it may be decomposed into subgroupings of the population, such as socioeconomic groups. This makes it possible for researchers to evaluate the contribution of each subgroup to overall inequality.

Computing the T measure is quite simple once a model of income distribution is selected. For example, the same output that produced the Gini coefficient for the data in table 7.6 will also show the mean equal to $62,845.71 and geometrical mean equal to $44,044.84. Hence $T = \ln(62,845.71/44,044.84) = 0.35547$.

An Inequality Measure Suggested by Atkinson

A. B. Atkinson [1] proposed a family of income inequality measures that are based on a society's social welfare function. The social welfare function makes the reasonable assumption that the collective utility of income for the population will be positively affected by an increasing mean income but negatively affected by increasing inequality of income. The general form of this family is given by:

$$A_\varepsilon = 1 - \left[\frac{1}{\mu_y^{1-\varepsilon}} \int_0^\infty y^{1-\varepsilon} f(y) dy \right]^{\frac{1}{1-\varepsilon}}, \quad \varepsilon > 0 \quad \text{and} \quad \varepsilon \neq 1,$$

where ε is the parameter that indexes the family of inequality measures. Parameter ε has a more subtle interpretation: Intuitively, it reflects society's tolerance for inequality. However, choosing ε requires a deep familiarity with the population being studied and requires methods that go beyond the level of this text. Therefore, we shall focus on the special case when $\varepsilon = 1$.

For $\varepsilon = 1$ the formula takes on the special form:

$$A_1 = 1 - \exp\left[\int_0^\infty \ln\left(\frac{y}{\mu_y}\right) f(y) dy \right]$$

$$= 1 - \exp\left[\int_0^\infty \ln(y) f(y) dy - \ln(\mu_y) \right]$$

$$= 1 - \frac{\mu_{gm}}{\mu_y}.$$

Hence the measure reduces to one minus the ratio of the geometric mean to the mean.

Problems

1. Estimate a Dagum model for U.S. families in 1998 using table 7.7. The age of householder for the above families is given in table 7.8. Compute the Paglin-Gini using the software package *P-Gini*.
2. For small discrete populations, the T measure may be written as:

$$T = \ln\left(\sum_{i=1}^n S_i Y_i\right) - \sum_{i=1}^n S_i \ln(Y_i),$$

Table 7.7 All Families Income Distribution, 1998

Income Bracket ($)	Number of Families (×1,000)
0–5,000	1,902
5,000–9,999	2,691
10,000–14,999	3,799
15,000–24,999	8,811
25,000–34,999	9,052
35,000–49,999	11,995
50,000–74,999	15,427
75,000–99,999	8,530
100,000+	9,524

where Y_i is the income of the ith income recipient in a population of n income recipients. S_i is the share of Y_i in total income of all income recipients. That is:

$$S_i = Y_i / \sum_{j=1}^{n} Y_j.$$

Suppose an island population consists of three individuals with incomes: $Y_1 = \$95$, $Y_2 = \$40$ and $Y_3 = \$15$.

a. Compute the T measure of inequality.
b. Increase each of the incomes by 20% and recompute the T measure.
c. Suppose $Y_1 = \$85$, $Y_2 = \$40$ and $Y_3 = \$25$, because the richest person gave $10 to the poorest person. Recompute the T measure.
d. Suppose $Y_1 = \$50$, $Y_2 = \$50$, and $Y_3 = \$50$. Recompute the T measure.

Table 7.8 Total Income of Families by Age of Householder, 1998

Age (years)	Number of Families	Mean Income ($)
15–24	3,242	30,124
25–34	13,226	48,598
35–44	18,823	63,925
45–54	15,127	75,582
55–64	9,635	68,425
65–74	7,025	50,110
75+	4,562	40,347

Source: U.S. Census Bureau, *Money Income in the United States: 1998* (P60-206), Washington, GPO, 1999.

3. Compute the Theil T and the Atkinson's A_1 inequality measures for U.S. families in 1998 (data in problem 1).

4. For small discrete populations, the Atkinson's A_1 inequality measure may be written as:

$$A_1 = 1 - \left\{ \exp\left[\sum_{i=1}^{n} S_i \ln(y_i)\right] \right\} / \mu_y, \text{ where } \mu_y = \sum_{i=1}^{n} S_i Y_i,$$

where Y_i is the income of the ith income recipient in a population of n income recipients. S_i is the share of Y_i in total income of all income recipients. That is:

$$S_i = Y_i / \sum_{j=1}^{n} Y_j.$$

Suppose an island population consists of three individuals with incomes $Y_1 = \$95$, $Y_2 = \$40$, and $Y_3 = \$15$.

a. Compute the A_1 measure of inequality.

b. Increase each of the incomes by 20% and recompute the A_1 measure.

c. Suppose $Y_1 = \$85$, $Y_2 = \$40$, and $Y_3 = \$25$, because the richest person gave $10 to the poorest person. Recompute the A_1 measure.

d. Suppose $Y_1 = \$50$, $Y_2 = \$50$, and $Y_3 = \$50$. Recompute the A_1 measure.

References

1. Atkinson, A. B., *On the Measurement of Inequality*, Journal of Economic Theory, Vol. 2, 1970, pp. 44–63.
2. Champernowne, D. G., *A Comparison of Measures of Inequality of Income Distribution*, Economic Journal, No. 84, 1975, pp. 787–816.
3. Champernowne, D. G. and F. A. Cowell, *Economic Equality and Income Distribution*, Cambridge, Cambridge University Press, 1999.
4. Danziger, Sheldon, Robert Haveman, and Eugene Smolensky, *The Measurement and Trend of Inequality: Comment*, American Economic Review, June 1977, pp. 505–512.
5. Formby, J. P. and Terry G. Seaks, *Paglin's Gini Measure of Inequality: A Modification*, American Economic Review, June 1980, pp. 479–482.
6. Formby, J. P., Terry G. Seaks, and W. James Smith, *On the Measurement and Trend of Inequality: A Reconsideration*, American Economic Review, March 1989, pp. 256–264.
7. Frosini, Benito V., *Comparing Inequality Measures*, Statistica, Vol. 45, No. 3, 1985, pp. 299–317.
8. Johnson, William R., *The Measurement and Trend of Inequality: Comment*, American Economic Review, June 1977, pp. 502–504.
9. Kakwani, Nanak C., *Income Inequality and Poverty*, A World Bank Research Publication, New York, Oxford University Press, 1980.

10. Kurien, C. John, *The Measurement and Trend of Inequality: Comment*, American Economic Review, June 1977, pp. 517–519.

11. Minarik, Joseph L., *The Measurement and Trend of Inequality: Comment*, American Economic Review, June 1977, pp. 513–516.

12. Nelson, Eric R., *The Measurement and Trend of Inequality: Comment*, American Economic Review, June 1977, pp. 497–501.

13. Paglin, Morton, *The Measurement and Trend of Inequality: A Basic Revision*, American Economic Review, September 1975, pp. 598–609.

14. Paglin, Morton, *The Measurement and Trend of Inequality: Reply*, American Economic Review, June 1977, pp. 520–531.

15. Pyatt, Graham, *On the Interpretation and Disaggregation of Gini Coefficients*, Economic Journal, June 1976, pp. 243–55.

16. Theil, Henri, *Economics and Information Theory*, Amsterdam, North-Holland, 1967.

17. Wertz, Kenneth L., *The Measurement and Trend of Inequality: Comment*, American Economic Review, Vol. 69, No. 4, September 1979, pp. 670–671.

8

Poverty

S ince the late 1950s, governments and international institutions
such as the United Nations, the World Bank, and many nongovernmental organizations have been deeply concerned with the state of human deprivation. In 1986 the Catholic Bishops of the United States issued a
document titled *Economic Justice for All, Catholic Social Teaching and the
U.S. Economy* [8]. Their main point was that while "there are many signs of
hope in the U.S. economic life today . . . these signs of hope are not the whole
story. There have been many failures." They point out, "Poor and homeless
people sleep in our church basements; the hungry line up in soup lines." Furthermore, "beyond our shores, the reality of 800 million people living in absolute poverty and 450 million malnourished or facing starvation casts an
ominous shadow over all these hopes and problems at home."

The poor are not a homogeneous group. There are populations of people
who are poor, all their ancestors were poor, and there is little expectation that
their children will be much better off. There are people who are on the poverty
threshold; in good times they are above the threshold, but in bad times they fall
below the threshold. Throughout the developing world, some of the most
affected casualties of poverty are women and children, victims of gender bias
and cultural practices that distribute the greatest share of household resources
to male householders.

In this chapter you will see how the income distribution models can contribute to the measurement of poverty.

8.1 Poverty Concepts

We generally like to distinguish between absolute poverty and relative poverty.
An extreme form of absolute poverty is when an income recipient cannot meet

basic needs. This is called *abject poverty*. Recall from chapter 1 that basic needs are those goods and services that are necessary to sustain life. Since this is the life-sustaining level of consumption, we argue that all income recipients have a right to basic needs, and no one should live in abject poverty.

However, most developed countries and some of the more advanced developing countries will view absolute poverty at a level above basic needs. A basket of goods and services is determined that sets the poverty threshold: That is, income recipients who have the basket of goods and services or more are not considered poor; those who do not are officially poor. The degree of poverty depends on how close the income recipient is to having the full basket. Since the basket is country specific, what might be considered poverty in one country, for example, the United States, may be a reasonably good standard of living in another country. Relative poverty within a country is related to income distribution. The bottom decile of income recipients may suffer from a feeling of income deprivation, whether or not they are below the official poverty threshold of the country.

Official Poverty Thresholds

In most countries, once the basket of goods and services that defines absolute poverty is defined, it is priced, and a threshold income is established that should be enough to buy the basket.

Table 8.1 shows the threshold incomes for different size families in the United States for the year 2000. These are the official poverty thresholds used to

Table 8.1 U.S. Poverty Thresholds by Family Size and Number of Related Children under the Age of 18 Years, 2000

Size of Family Unit	Related Children under 18 Years								
	0	1	2	3	4	5	6	7	8+
1 Person									
Under 65 Years	8,959								
65 Years +	8,259								
2 People									
Householder under 65	11,531	11,869							
Householder 65 +	10,409	11,824							
3 People	13,470	13,861	13,874						
4 People	17,761	18,052	17,463	17,524					
5 People	21,419	21,731	21,065	20,550	20,236				
6 People	24,636	24,734	24,224	23,736	23,009	22,579			
7 People	28,347	28,524	27,914	27,489	26,696	25,772	24,758		
8 People	31,704	31,984	31,408	30,904	30,188	29,279	28,334	28,093	
9 People or More	38,138	38,322	37,813	37,385	36,682	35,716	34,841	34,625	33,291

Source: U.S. Census Bureau, *Poverty in the United States: 2000* (P60–214), Washington, GPO, 2001.

estimate the number of poor people and to determine eligibility for government aid to poor families. Families whose incomes are above the number for their size are not considered poor; those with incomes below are poor. The numbers are estimated under the assumption that poor families spend one third of their gross income on food. The basket of food that is on the threshold of poverty is determined by the Department of Agriculture. Once the value of the food basket is determined, it is multiplied by three, and the income threshold is established.

Another implicit assumption is that if families have enough income to buy the poverty threshold basket, they will. This may or may not be the case. For example, the food basket that is determined by the U.S. Department of Agriculture (*The Economy Food Plan*) is designed to provide the necessary nutrients for a healthy diet. However, it has been estimated that families whose food budget is at the cost of the Economy Food Plan have only about a 1 in 2 chance of getting a fair or better diet, and only 1 chance in 10 of getting a good diet (see Fisher [4]).

One difficulty with estimating income poverty thresholds in terms of a basket of consumption, whether the basket is based only on food or on non-food items as well, is that prices may be subject to geographical location. If, for example, the cost of the basket varies between urban and rural areas, then defining poverty in terms of the same income poverty threshold is inconsistent. Differences in urban and rural lifestyles may also affect the basket itself. Urbanites may require more formal and more expensive clothing. Rural people engaged in heavy manual labor such as farming may require more protein and caloric intake. One consumption basket and one threshold income may not be appropriate for an entire nation.

Ravallion and Bidani [6] make the point that the real expenditure level at which an urban resident typically attains any given caloric requirement will tend to be higher than in rural areas because of a difference in tastes. In the Philippines separate poverty thresholds were established for 12 regions of the country (see Intal and Bantilan [5]) at two levels, the absolute poverty threshold and the basic needs subsistence threshold. Food menus were differentiated by region and urban-rural within region. The resulting income thresholds for 1991 are shown in table 8.2.

Estimating the Number of Poor Income Recipients

When the poverty threshold is expressed in money terms, it is possible to estimate the number of poor income recipients below the threshold. Such estimates are sometimes called *head-counts*. Since the degree of poverty will vary under the threshold, it is useful to be able to estimate some statistics of the income recipients who are poor. For example, it is useful to know the mean income of those below the income threshold and to be able to estimate the number of income recipients below subthreshold incomes.

Table 8.2 Per Capita Absolute Poverty and Basic Needs Thresholds (1991 Nominal Pesos)

Region	1	2	3	4	5	6	7	8	9	10	11	12
Absolute Poverty	8,123	7,072	8,293	8,083	6,476	6,545	5,650	5,240	6,957	6,564	6,529	6,913
Basic Needs		5,311	4,811	5,402	5,422	4,433	4,426	3,988	3,894	4,270	4,494	4,660	4,499

	Manila Region
Absolute Poverty	9,471
Basic Needs	5,757

Region: 1, Ilocos; 2, Cagayan Valley; 3, Central Luzon; 4, Southern Tagalog; 5, Bicol; 6, West Visayas; 7, Central Visayas; 8, East Visayas; 9, West Mindanao; 10, North Mindanao; 11, South Mindanao; 12, Central Mindanao.

Source: Intal, P. S. and M. C. S. Bantilan, *Understanding Poverty and Inequality in the Philippines*, Manila, National Economic and Development Authority and United Nations Development Program, 1994.

If we let $Y_{pov}=$ the threshold income, and $N_{pov}=$ the number of poor income recipients in a population of N income recipients, then it follows:

$$N_{pov} = F\,(Y_{pov}) \times N,$$

where $F(Y)$ is the cumulative distribution function of the income density function. The total income flowing to all those below the threshold is given by:

$$Ytotal_{pov} = N \cdot \int_0^{Y_{pov}} g(y)dy, \text{ where } g(y) = yf(y).$$

The mean income of those below the poverty threshold is then:

$$\mu_{pov} = Ytotal_{pov}/N_{pov}.$$

To measure the inequality among the poor, we compute a Gini coefficient for only the income recipients below the poverty threshold.

$$Gini_{pov} = 2\,\frac{\int_0^{Y_{pov}} g(y)F(y)dy}{F(y_{pov})G(y_{pov})} - 1, \text{ where } g(y)=yf(y) \text{ and}$$

$$G(y_{pov}) = \int_0^{Y_{pov}} g(y)dy.$$

As an example, the data in table 8.3 give the income distribution of three-person U.S. families with only 1 child (the child is less than 18 years old and living at home). The data were fitted to the Champernowne model, and the following parameters were found:

$$\vartheta = .29073 \times 10^{-9}, \ \alpha = 3.2466, \ Y_0 = 76.934, \text{ and } \sigma = .66018.$$

These were then input into software package *CDF_CHAM* along with the total population ($N = 10,188$) and the poverty threshold $Y_{pov} = 13.861$. The program estimated that the percent of families below the poverty threshold is 2.98%, that is, $N_{pov} = .298 \times 10,188 = 3,036.024 \times 1,000$ families. It also

Table 8.3 Three-Person 1-Child Families in the
United States, 2000

Income Class ($)	Number of Families (thousands)
0–5,000	66
5,000–10,000	115
10,000–15,000	176
15,000–25,000	614
25,000–35,000	846
35,000–50,000	1,556
50,000–75,000	2,691
75,000–100,000	1,690
100 +	2,434

Source: U.S. Census Bureau, *Current Population Survey Annual Demographic Survey*, Washington, GPO, March Supplement 2000.

estimated the mean income of the families below the threshold as $9.435×1,000. Hence the head-count of 3-person families (with 1 child below the age of 18) below the poverty threshold is 3,036,024, and their mean income is $9,435 for the year 2000. The Gini coefficient among the poor, that is, the amount of inequality among those people below the poverty threshold as measured by the Gini coefficient, is .191.

Relative Poverty

Relative poverty is closely linked with income inequality. Consider the case of an attorney employed as a clerk in the state court system. As a civil servant, her salary will be far less than her classmate who is employed as an attorney in a large law firm. She may feel relatively deprived, although officially she is not absolutely poor.

During periods of high growth, as the 1992 to 2000 period in the United States, it sometimes happens that the Gini coefficient increases. However, as we see in table 8.4, during the same period in the United States, the number of families below the poverty threshold decreased. Hence, relative poverty

Table 8.4 U.S. Gini Coefficient and Number of Families Below the Poverty Level

Year	1992	1993	1994	1995	1996	1997	1998	1999	2000
Gini	.434	.454	.456	.450	.455	.459	.456	.457	.460
Percent Families Below Poverty Level	13.3	13.6	13.1	12.3	12.2	11.6	11.2	10.2	9.6

Sources: U.S. Census Bureau, *Money Income in the United States: 2000* (P60–213), Washington, GPO, 2001; U.S. Census Bureau, *Poverty in the United States: 2000* (P60–214), Washington, GPO, 2001.

increased, while absolute poverty decreased. Another way of saying this is: The rich got richer, the poor got richer, but the rich got richer faster. This can work in reverse. It might happen during a slowdown of the economy that relative poverty decreases as absolute poverty increases.

Since relative poverty is unavoidable as long as there is a tolerance for inequality of income, most governments are not concerned with it unless inequality is so extreme that it is the cause of absolute poverty. In the case where relative poverty reflects static income mobility, it can be a major cause of political instability, and sooner or later policy makers make efforts to correct it.

Except for the last few centuries, in almost every country of the world, there has been an underclass of people who were born relatively poor and who have had almost no chance of changing their income status. While that situation still exists *de facto* today in some countries, most countries offer some way to improve the lifetime income status of the children of low-income families. The normal route is through free public education, but in some developing countries the children of the poorest families may elevate their status through other routes, such as a career in the military or in sports.

8.2 Alternative Poverty Measures

Although the head-count measure of poverty is the most widely used poverty summary measure, it is deficient on two accounts. One criticism is that it defines poverty too sharply. An income recipient whose annual income is one unit of currency above the poverty threshold is not poor, while a neighbor who had an income of one unit of currency less for the year is poor. Second, it does not indicate the degree of relative poverty among the poor income recipients.

A number of alternative summary poverty measures have been proposed that address some of these weaknesses in the head-count method, but they do not all indicate the same trends in poverty across groups or over time. This is important because governments want to know whether their policies are effective in reducing the amount of poverty (see Atkinson [1]).

A selection of some of the more important alternative poverty measures is given below. These are taken from those suggested by Blackwood and Lynch [3].

The Income Shortfall

This type of measure is related to the amount of income that would have to be transferred to the poor in order to bring all income recipients below the poverty threshold up to the threshold. This can be accomplished by estimating the amount of additional income needed or by estimating the average amount of additional income needed.

$$Y_{shortfall} = N_{pov}(Y_{pov} - \mu_{pov}).$$

To get the average shortfall, simply divide $Y_{shortfall}$ by N_{pov}. Another variant is to compute the ratio of the income shortfall to the poverty threshold.

Sen's Poverty Measure

A. K. Sen [7] proposed a poverty measure that incorporates the Gini coefficient computed for income recipients below the poverty threshold, the headcount ratio (N_{pov}/N), and the mean income of those below the poverty threshold.

$$S = F(Y_{pov}) \left[\frac{Y_{pov} - \mu_{pov}(1 - Gini_{pov})}{Y_{pov}} \right].$$

Since $F(Y_{pov}) = N_{pov}/N$, Sen's poverty measure may be written in the alternative form:

$$S = \frac{N_{pov}}{N} \left[\frac{Y_{pov} - \mu_{pov}(1 - Gini_{pov})}{Y_{pov}} \right]$$
$$= \frac{N_{pov}}{N} \left[\frac{Y_{pov} - \mu_{pov} + \mu_{pov} Gini_{pov}}{Y_{pov}} \right].$$

If no one is below the poverty threshold, then the head-count ratio will be 0, and S will also be 0. From the above equation, we see that S will increase if the number of poor income recipients increases or if the inequality between them increases. Hence transfers of income between poor income recipients can make the measure increase or decrease, depending on whether it is a regressive or a progressive transfer. In this sense, Sen's index captures the *weak law of transfers*, one of the desirable traits of inequality and poverty measures.

The desirability of the weak law of transfers is based on the assumption that there is a declining marginal utility for income, even among the poor. If there is a transfer of income between two poor income recipients, the better-off of the two should have a lower marginal utility for income than the other. When the transfer is from the better-off income recipient to the other, there is a net gain in utility, and welfare increases. On the other hand, if the transfer is from the poorer income recipient to the better-off one, then there is a net loss of utility, and welfare decreases. This is consistent with Pareto optimality.

Another feature of Sen's poverty measure is that when the Gini coefficient among the income recipients below the poverty threshold is 0—that is, when all poor income recipients have the same income—the index is reduced and directly proportional to the average income shortfall. This feature has this important policy implication: In the process of alleviating poverty, priority should be given to the poorest of the poor first until all the poor are at the same level of income.

Table 8.5 All Married Couple Families in the United
States, 2000

Income Class ($)	Number of Families (thousands)
0–5,000	587
5,000–10,000	748
10,000–15,000	1,632
15,000–25,000	4,929
25,000–35,000	5,947
35,000–50,000	8,754
50,000–75,000	13,231
75,000–100,000	8,247
100+	11,537
Total	55,612

Source: U.S. Census Bureau, *Current Population Survey Annual
Demographic Survey*, Washington, GPO, March Supplement 2000.

We will use the estimates computed for the 3-person 1-child families in the
United States for the year 2000 to demonstrate the ease in computing Sen's
poverty measure. From the above we get:

$Y_{pov} = 13,861$, $F(Y_{pov}) = .298$, $Gini_{pov} = .191$, and $\mu_{pov} = 9,435$.

Substituting these into the formula:

$$S = .298 \left[\frac{13,861 - 9,435(1 - .191)}{13,861} \right] = .1339.$$

Table 8.6 Family Income in the Philippines, 1991

Income Class (P)	Total Number of Families
0–10,000	307
10,000–19,999	1,648
20,000–29,999	2,145
30,000–39,999	1,732
40,000–49,999	1,251
50,000–59,999	979
60,000–79,999	1,235
80,000–99,999	773
100,000–149,999	1,018
150,000–249,999	594
250,000–499,999	237
500,000+	60
Total	1,979

Source: National Statistical Office, 1991 FIES, Manila, Philippines.

Problems

1. Use the Dagum model and software package *CDF_DAG* to estimate the number of U.S. married couple families with income less than $14,000. The data are shown in table 8.5.
2. Estimate a Dagum model for the Philippines 1991 income data given in table 8.6. The average low-income Filipino family in 1991 had 5.5 members. Use software package *CDF_DAG* to estimate the percentage of income families below the lowest basic needs threshold of $5.5 \times 4,500 = 24,750$ pesos. What is their mean income? What is the Gini coefficient among the poor? *Reminder*: Do not forget to scale income by dividing by 1,000 when using the Dagum model.
3. Compute Sen's poverty measure for problem 2.

References

1. Atkinson, A. B., *On the Measure of Poverty*, Econometrica, Vol. 55, No. 4, July 1987, pp. 749–764.
2. Blackorby, Charles and David Donaldson, *Ethical Indices for the Measure of Poverty*, Econometrica, Vol. 48, No. 4, May 1980, pp. 1053–1060.
3. Blackwood, D. L. and R. G. Lynch, *The Measurement of Inequality and Poverty: A Policy Maker's Guide to the Literature*, World Development, Vol. 22, No. 4, 1994, pp. 567–578.
4. Fisher, Gordon M., *The Development and History of the Poverty Thresholds*, Social Security Bulletin, Vol. 55, No. 4, 1992, pp. 1–24.
5. Intal Jr., P. S. and M. C. S. Bantilan, *Understanding Poverty and Inequality in the Philippines*, Manila, National Economic and Development Authority and United Nations Development Program, 1994.
6. Ravallion, Martin and Benu Bidani, *How Robust is the Poverty Profile?*, World Bank Economic Review, Vol. 8, No. 1, 1994, pp. 75–102.
7. Sen, A. K., *Poverty: an Ordinal Approach to Measurement*, Econometrica, Vol. 44, March, 1976, 219–231.
8. United States Catholic Conference, *Economic Justice for All: Catholic Social Teaching and the U.S. Economy*, Third Draft, Publication No. 998, Washington, June 1986.

9

Country Comparisons

A t the end of World War II, economic attention was focused on the rebuilding of those countries that were destroyed in the conflict. The economic miracles of Germany and Japan, as well as the success of the Marshall Plan in Europe, encouraged economists to try similar strategies with the developing countries, many of which were recently independent ex-colonies.

In the 1960s the United Nations launched the first developing decade aimed at increasing growth of GDP of the developing countries. This was followed by the second developing decade in the 1970s and the third in the 1980s. The results were not as spectacular as the experience with the Marshall Plan. There were many disappointments, and each decade's experience ended with many questions about the approach of the strategy and what might be done to achieve more favorable results in the next strategy.

One of the first questions to be dealt with was, What are the macroeconomic characteristics of a developing country? How do you draw the line between a developing country and a developed country? For example, should Argentina be considered a developing or a developed country. Before the war, Argentina and Japan were at about the same level.

The first developing decade settled on letting per capita GDP be the main indicator of level of development. This was based on the correlation between many things found in the rich countries, such as telephones, level of education and health services, and per capita GDP. It was believed that if per capita GDP could accelerate, then all the other accruements of the developed countries would automatically follow. However, in some countries, growth of per capita GDP only made a small proportion of the population well off, leaving most people behind in the traditional economy. Income distribution worsened.

In this chapter you will learn how international institutions and some internationally minded academics developed measures of relative development between countries.

9.1 Assessing the Standard of Living between Countries

The World Bank, the United Nations, UNESCO (United Nations Educational, Scientific, and Cultural Organization), the World Health Organization, and other international institutions periodically produce tables of statistics to compare countries. Comparisons are made on the status of socioeconomic variables such as population, health, education, national debt, and level of development. Such comparisons, while they are interesting in themselves, are necessary for the governing bodies of these institutions because they help in the formulation of intergovernmental policies and decisions that involve billions of dollars of aid between developed and developing countries.

The raw data, which are the basis of these statistics, originate in the statistical offices of each country. In some cases, when a developing country does not have the expertise or the means to produce a data series required by an international institution, a team of experts is sent by the institution to the country to help them produce what is needed. Of great interest to the international institutions is the relative standard of living between countries.

Per Capita Income Tables

Annual per capita income tables are included in the data series of all international institutions. They are generally published in a yearly report along with other variables pertaining to the organization's specialized interests. Per capita income is computed by dividing each country's GDP by its total population.

In order to compare per capita income between countries, it is necessary to use a common currency for the countries being compared. Quite frequently, U.S. dollars are used for this purpose. When comparisons are made through time as well as across countries, then *real* or *constant* units of currency must be used. That is, the effects of inflation are removed between years by deflating GDP by a price index, which will put all years in the prices of one year called the base year. The selection of the base year is somewhat arbitrary, but it is generally a good practice to use a more recent year for this purpose; otherwise, the per capita figures will appear too low and outdated.

Table 9.1 gives a comparison of GDP per capita by major regions of the world and some selected countries. Comparisons are also made for 2 years, 1980 and 1998. Values of per capita GDP are given in 1993 prices. The developed countries, which only had less than 15% of the world's population in 1998, had an income of $25,649 per person, while the developing countries

Table 9.1 Population and GDP Per Capita

	Population (millions)		GDP Per Capita (real 1993 U.S.$)	
	1980	1998	1980	1998
World	4,367	5,813	4,078	4,789
Developed Countries	756	839	18,184	25,649
United States	230	274	20,551	28,313
European Union	355	374	15,041	20,838
Japan	117	126	23,483	35,873
Transition Economies	378	411	2,261	1,206
Developing Countries	3,233	4,564	993	1,278
Latin America	354	411	3,262	3,395
Africa	455	746	786	663
Sub-Saharan Africa	262	440	438	353
West Asia	137	235	6,224	3,502
East Asia	2,287	3,090	369	920
China	981	1,233	181	777
South Asia	892	1,289	213	358
Least-Developed Countries	379	600	282	258

Source: United Nations, *World Economic Survey 1999*, New York.

with over 78% of the population only had a per capita income of $1,278. Furthermore, the 600 million people living in the least-developed countries had only $258 per person, or about one-hundredth of the income per person of the developed countries.

The least-developed countries are generally defined in terms of per capita GDP; however, other variables, which are often highly correlated with per capita GDP, are also important. Social variables such as population growth rate, life expectancy, illiteracy rates, health and sanitation access, and housing give a more complete description of the least-developed countries. Most of these countries are also plagued by social tensions and civil war and a structure of production that has 30% to 40% of GDP originating out of inefficient traditional agriculture.

While the per capita incomes of these countries are very low, they do not tell the whole income story. Income distribution studies done in these countries indicate that the bottom (poorest) 40% of the people are often living in abject poverty. For example, the World Bank [5] estimated that Bangladesh had a GDP per capita of U.S. $220 in 1993. The population was estimated at 115,203,000 people. Thus, the GDP was $2,534,460,000. However, they also estimated that the poorest 40% of the population only had 23% of the GDP. Hence, their per capita income was only $126. Furthermore, the poorest 20% only had 10% of the GDP. Their per capita income was $110.

One example of the importance of per capita income for international organizations is its use by the Poverty Reduction and Growth Facility of the International Monetary Fund (IMF). Established in 1999, this program of the IMF lends developing countries, which have per capita incomes less than $875 (current 2001 U.S. dollars) very low interest loans to integrate the objectives of poverty reduction and GDP growth. Currently, there are about 71 countries that are eligible for such loans. To obtain the loan, a country must prepare a *Poverty Reduction Strategy Paper* that indicates the country's plan to further peace, democracy, and effective governance, as well as promote social justice, education, health, and economic growth in the private sector.

Purchasing Power Parity

While it may be possible for some people to survive on $258 a year in the least-developed countries, it would not be possible in the United States. The market exchange rates between the United States and the least-developed countries do not reflect cost-of-living differences. In 1968 the United Nations launched the International Comparisons Programme in order to get a better estimate of the purchasing power parity (PPP) between countries. The project was established at the University of Pennsylvania under the directorship of Irving Kravis, who was soon joined by Alan Heston. A few years later, Robert Summers joined the team. Since then the team has been sampling prices of goods and services for typical consumption baskets in a number countries scattered throughout the world.

The countries include both developed and developing, but the samples are conducted only periodically for "benchmark" years. Methods have been developed to interpolate comparable real GDP in international prices for the in-between years. The PPPs are computed for each component of the expenditure table of the national accounts in each country studied; that is, there is a PPP for private consumption, for government, for investment (gross fixed capital formation), and one for net exports. We can see this by recalling the national accounts identity:

$$\text{GDP} = Y = C + G + I + (X - M),$$

where GDP is gross domestic product, C is private consumption, G is government, I is investment, X is exports, and M is imports. The PPP for Y is then given by:

$$PPP_Y = w_c PPP_c + w_G PPP_G + w_I PPP_I + w_{x-m} PPP_{x-m}.$$

The weights are proportional to the share of the component in GDP; hence the most important is w_c, which is the weight of private consumption. The private consumption PPP is derived from the weighted average of 31 PPPs broadly classified into: Food, Beverages and Tobacco; Clothing and Footwear;

Gross Rents, Fuel and Power; Household Equipment and Operation; Medical Care; Transportation and Communication; Recreation and Education; Miscellaneous Goods and Services; and Net Purchases from abroad.

In the case of the Philippines, the PPP_Y for the benchmark year 1985 turned out to be 6.297 pesos for U.S. $1. The IMF market exchange rate (rf—periodic averages) for 1985 was 18.607 pesos to U.S. $1. In local currency, the per capita income was 11,280 pesos. Using the IMF exchange rate to U.S. dollars yields $606 per capita. However, when the PPP is applied, the per capita figure increases to $1,791. The latter figure is a much better comparison of living standards. Incidentally, the per capita income in the United States was $16,494, which is about 9 times the per capita of the Philippines using international prices; but using the market exchange rate, it would be about 27 times the Philippine amount.

The difficulty with using market exchange rates for international comparisons is that they do not reflect domestic purchasing power but, rather, the terms of trade, the international debt situation of the country, and interest rate differentials between the country and major trading partners. It is rather easy to use international price comparisons because they are available online through the Penn World Table (PWT), which can be accessed at http://www.ssc .upenn.edu/cgi-bin/pwt/pwtView.pl.

The basic needs threshold for a family of five was about 25,000 pesos in the Philippines during 1992. One useful exercise is to convert this amount into international prices using the Penn World Tables. This can be done by accessing the table and requesting the real GDP/capita (current international prices)[1] for 1992. If this is done, the computer system will give 2,172. To get the implicit PPP converter, divide the per capita income in local currency by 2,172. That is:

$$GDP/capita(local\ currency) = 1{,}351{,}600/64.259$$
$$= 21{,}033.63\ pesos.$$

The implicit PPP is then $21{,}033.63/2{,}172 = 9.684$, and the basic needs threshold in international prices is $25{,}000/9.684$, or about 2,582 real/current international prices.

Sometimes it is necessary to estimate the number of income recipients below an income threshold for a group of countries. One way to do this is to standardize the units across countries by converting each country's income distribution into international prices before estimating the income distribution models. Likewise, the income threshold should also be put in international prices before the program is used, to estimate the number of people below the threshold.

---

[1]There are a number of choices of units offered by the PWT. For the purposes of the exercises that we will be doing in this text, we will use real GDP (current international prices).

As an example, suppose we want to estimate the number of families with yearly income less than $14,000 (1995 U.S. dollars) in both Canada and the United States during the year 1995. Using the Penn World Table 6.0 (PWT6), U.S. $14,000 converts into 7,715 real GDP/current international prices. The 1995 family income distributions for Canada and the United States are given in table 9.2.

First we will estimate an income distribution model for the United States in 1995 dollars. The best fit was obtained using the Champernowne model, which yielded parameters:

$$\vartheta = 5.917, \ \alpha = 3.0959, \ Y_o = 59,145, \ \text{and} \ \sigma = .53089.$$

The above fit estimates the Gini coefficient at .4092. The next step is to input these parameters into program *CDF_CHAM*. When the program prompts for the total population, input 100 because the distribution is given in terms of percents of families and not numbers of families. *CDF_CHAM* returned 11.2% of families had income less than $14,000. Since the total number of families in the United States in 1995 was 69,597,000, the number with income less than $14,000 is estimated to be $.112 \times 69,597,000 = 7,794,864$ families.

Canada must be put into real/current international prices. To do this, we request the 1995 real per capita income/current international prices for Canada from the PWT6. The number in the PWT6 is 22,417. The per capita income for 1995 in Canadian dollars was $50,458. Hence the ratio $22,417/50,458 = .4106956$ is used to multiply the income class endpoints of the Canadian income distribution

Table 9.2 Family Income Distributions for Canada and the United States, 1995

Canada		United States	
Income Brackets ($)	% of Families	Income Brackets ($)	% of Families
0–10,000	5.6	0–5,000	2.4
10,000–20,000	10.2	5,000–10,000	4.1
20,000–30,000	12.9	10,000–15,000	5.8
30,000–40,000	12.7	15,000–25,000	13.0
40,000–50,000	12.4	25,000–35,000	13.4
50,000–60,000	11.3	35,000–50,000	17.6
60,000–70,000	9.4	50,000–75,000	21.2
70,000–80,000	7.2	75,000–100,000	11.0
80,000–100,000	9.0	100,000 +	11.4
100,000–125,000	5.1		
125,000–150,000	2.0		
150,000 +	2.4		
Total Number of Families	7,837,865	69,597,000	

Sources: Statistics Canada, *The Nation* series: Package No. 9, catalog no. 93F0029XDB96000, Ottawa 1998; U.S. Census Bureau, *Money Income in the United States: 1999* (PCO-209), Washington, GPO, 2000.

Table 9.3 Canadian Family Income Distribution
in Real/Current International Prices, 1995

Income Brackets ($)	Percent of Families
0–4,107	5.6
4,107–8,214	10.2
8,214–12,321	12.9
12,321–16,428	12.7
16,428–20,535	12.4
20,535–24,642	11.3
24,642–28,745	9.4
28,975–32,856	7.2
32,856–41,070	9.0
41,070–51,337	5.1
51,337–61,604	2.0
61,604+	2.4

to convert them into real/current international prices for 1995. The result is shown in table 9.3.

Table 9.3 was fitted to the Dagum model, which proved to be the best for this distribution. The resulting parameters were:

$$\alpha = .5001 \times 10^{-9}, \ \lambda = 329{,}450, \ \delta = 3.7411, \quad \text{and} \quad \beta = .38232.$$

Note that in using the Dagum model the income bracket endpoints were scaled down by dividing them by 1,000. The Gini came out to be .3658. These parameters and the threshold of 7,715 (U.S. $14,000 in 1995) were input into CDF_DAG, and 14.4% was returned as the percent of families below the threshold. Since the total number of families is 7,837,865, the total number of Canadian families below $14,000 is estimated to be 1,129,436. The grand total for both Canada and the United States is then $1{,}129{,}436 + 7{,}794{,}864 = 8{,}924{,}300$.

The Human Development Index

In 1990, the United Nations Development Program (UNDP) introduced the Human Development Index (HDI). This index was their first attempt to measure the progress of countries' efforts to take into account social objectives as well as growth of GDP in assessing development.

The HDI incorporates the country's life expectancy, educational index, and per capita GDP (purchasing power parity in U.S. dollars) into an index. The educational index is derived from the literacy rate and the gross enrollment rate. Life expectancy is used as a proxy for general health-care development. Each of these three components of the index is given the same weight, but per capita income is put in natural logarithms. The maximum and minimum of each measure over all countries are determined. Then, for every country, each component

Table 9.4 Maximum and Minimum Values of HDI Index

Indicator	Maximum Value	Minimum Value
Life Expectancy at Birth	85	25
Adult Literacy Rate (%)	100	0
Combined Gross Enrolment Ratio (%)	100	0
GDP Per Capita (PPP U.S.$)	40,000	100

of the index is standardized between 0 and 1 by using ratios that subtract the minimum value of the measure of the lowest country from the country's value and dividing this by the maximum value minus the minimum value.

For example, suppose the maximum and minimum values for a particular year are as given in table 9.4. Then if a country has a life expectancy of 47.8, an adult literacy of 46.7, a gross enrollment rate of 38.0, and a per capita income in PPP U.S. dollars of $1,630, the components are computed as follows:

Life expectancy component: $(47.8 - 25)/(85 - 25) = 0.38$
Adult literacy: $(46.7 - 0)/(100 - 0) = .467$
Gross enrollment: $(38 - 0)/(100 - 0) = .38$
Education component: $2/3(.467) + 1/3(.38) = .439$
GDP component: $[\ln(1,630) - \ln(100)]/[\ln(40,000) - \ln(100)] = .466$

The final HDI for the country is: $(.38 + .439 + .466)/3 = .428$.

9.2 Quantile Comparisons

The World Bank, as well as a number of other international organizations, publishes income distribution comparisons between countries using income

Table 9.5 Share of Income Flowing to the Top 20% of Households, the Bottom 40% of Households, and the Bottom 20% of Households

Household Group	Low Income		Middle Income		High Income	
	Ethiopia	China	Brazil	Mexico	United States	Canada
Top 20%	41	42	68	56	46	42
Bottom 40%	21	17	7	12	15	17
Bottom 20%	9	6	2	4	4	5
Ratio of Top 20% to Bottom 20%	4.5	7.0	34.0	14.0	11.5	8.4

Sources: For low- and middle-income countries: World Bank, *Social Indicators of Development 1995*, Baltimore, Md., Johns Hopkins University Press, 1995. For the United States and Canada, see references in table 9.2.

shares of different quantiles of the population. For example, *Social Indicators of Development*, a yearbook published by the World Bank, contains the share of household income flowing to the top 20% of households, the bottom 40% of households, and the bottom 20% of households.

Table 9.5 illustrates how quantile distributions may be used for between-country comparisons. Six countries have been selected, 2 of which can be classified as low income because they have relatively low per capita incomes, 2 middle income, and 2 high income. In each category, 1 of the countries has more of a social welfare orientation than the other. These are China, Mexico, and Canada.

When we examine the ratio of shares of the top 20% of households to the bottom 20% of households, we notice that they tend to be higher for the middle-income countries than for the low- and high-income countries. This raises the the interesting question of whether this is generally true; that is, in the process of development from low levels of per capita GDP to higher levels, does income inequality worsen and then improve again? A secondary question is, To what extent can government transfers to the bottom 20% improve the living conditions of the poorer households? We will take up these questions in subsequent chapters, but it suffices to say here that both of these questions are the focus of considerable debate.

Problems

1. The Republic of the Philippines had a GDP of about 266,228 million (current international units) in 2000. The population was about 76 million people. Hence the per capita income was about 3,500 current international units. Suppose the population continues to grow at the current rate, which is about 2.3%, and the economy can grow at a potential of about 4.5%. In what year would you expect it to achieve a per capita income of 20,000 current international units, which is about what the United States was in 1985? *Hint*: The per capita growth rate under this scenario is $4.5 - 2.3 = 2.2\%$.

2. Referring to problem 1, what would the growth rate of GDP have to be for the Philippines to reach 20,000 current international units in 2050?

3. Using the Champernowne model estimated for the U.S. data given in table 9.2 and the Dagum model estimated for Canada in table 9.3, estimate the percentage of families in the United States and Canada with incomes between $14,000 and $50,000.

4. Using the Dagum model estimated for the Philippines in problem 2, chapter 8, find the quintile distribution of income and compute the ratio of the share of income of the top 20% to the bottom 20%.

References

1. Kravis, I. B., Z. Kenessey, A. Heston, and R. Summers, *A System of International Comparisons of Gross Product and Purchasing Power*, Baltimore, Md., Johns Hopkins University Press, 1975.
2. International Monetary Fund, *The IMF's Poverty Reduction and Growth Facility (PRGF)*, Factsheet, September 2002.
3. United Nations, *Enhancing Socio-Economic Policies in the Least Developed Countries of Asia*, New York, United Nations, 1999.
4. United Nations Development Programme, *Human Development Report 2002*, New York, Oxford University Press, 2002.
5. World Bank, *Social Indicators of Development 1995*, Baltimore, Md., Johns Hopkins University Press, 1995.

10

Economic Development and Income Distribution

Almost every political leader dreams of an economic adviser who can recommend an economic strategy that will result in high GDP growth with equity. The connection between economic development and income distribution is tenuous, to say the least. While this connection has been substantially researched for as long as there has been an economics profession, neither economic theory nor empirical research has yet provided the exact linkage between the two. However, the economics profession is still young, and perhaps as it gains a longer data bank of economic history, some of the controversy that surrounds the issues will be resolved, and future economic advisers will be able to spell out a prescription for equitable economic growth.

10.1 The Controversy

Any discussion of the relationship between economic development and income distribution (if one exists) should first begin with what measure of development would be most appropriate. Early empirical studies focused on per capita income as the proxy for the level of development, but we know from chapter 9 that growth of GDP, especially when market exchange rates are used in international comparisons, may be misleading. This is especially true for the least-developed countries.

Another problem for empirical research is the lack of income distribution surveys, not only in the developing countries but also in the developed countries. It is virtually impossible to do any longitudinal studies because comparable surveys do not exist (not even in the United States) over a long enough period of economic development to discern any trends. Much of the empirical research has been based on cross-country analysis, which is subject to differences in the quality of data between countries as well as differences resulting from different definitions of income and income recipient.

The main questions in regard to the relationship between economic development and income distribution are:

1. Does the growth process have any influence on changes in the income distribution independent of government intervention?
2. If the answer to the above is yes, are there any stages of development that cause inequality to increase? If so, will the inequality offset any gains that the poorer populations may have gotten as a consequence of development?

James K. Galbraith [10] of the University of Texas listed four possible connections between growth and income distribution:

i. The *redistribution view*, which agrees with the endogenous growth school conclusion that development takes place most swiftly if emphasis is placed on social as well as economic development. That is education, health, and an institutional environment that encourages research and development of internationally traded products will lead to a faster and more equitable distribution of the benefits of growth. This is essentially the model that the fast-growing Asian countries have followed.

ii. The *neoliberal view*, which stresses export-oriented growth and technological change. The difference between this approach and the redistribution view is that in this case social development is not a precondition for economic growth but may result as the benefits of growth "trickle down" to those at the bottom of the society. In this process, income inequality may arise, but those at the bottom eventually will have increasing incomes.

iii. The *Kuznets and Keynes view*, which implies that increasing income inequality may occur as development takes place, but this may be offset with social welfare policies. As more of the population is employed in the modern sectors of the economy, the income inequality will begin to reverse itself, especially if there is some redistribution through social welfare policies.

iv. The *Scotch Verdict*—"not proven"—is that there may not be any connection between development and income distribution, at least not any in a systematic way.

Which, if any, of these views is correct? It is hard to say, mainly because of the inadequacies of the data. However, much of the controversy is centered around view iii. Therefore, we will look at the debate that is centered around the Kuznets "inverted U-shaped hypothesis" first.

The Kuznets "Inverted U-Shaped Hypothesis"

Simon Kuznets was one of the first people to explore the relationship between economic growth and income distribution. In a landmark study published in 1955 [13], he formulated the hypothesis that the least developed of the developing countries, that is, those whose economies are mainly in the traditional sector (agriculture), generally will have a more even income distribution than those developing countries that are more advanced in modernizing their economies.

The basic reasoning behind this is that wages in the modern sector will be substantially higher than in the traditional sector, thereby creating greater inequality. However, when the former developing country becomes developed, and the modern sector dominates the economy, most of the population will depend on income from the modern sector and the income distribution will tend toward more equality. This has become the "inverted U-shaped hypothesis."

In a follow-up 1963 empirical study [14], he posed two questions:

1. Do changes in the scope and structure of the production process that accompany economic growth and constitute its essence also affect the distribution of the growing income among the population?
2. Does the distribution of income, thus affected by the process of modern growth, have in turn an effect on the latter—by influencing not only consumption and savings but also the contribution of the income recipients to national product?

This study was based on a small database of 20 observations.[1] Kuznets was much concerned with the limitations of the data and devoted about 20 pages of the 80-page study to the problems associated with definitions, measurement, and coverage. His concluding remarks begin with:

With due allowance for the incompleteness of coverage, the empirical findings can be summarized briefly.

(a) The size distribution of income among families or consuming units today is more unequal in the less developed countries than in the developed countries. . . .

(b) . . . the distribution of income in the underdeveloped countries and in many developed countries is less unequal in the agricultural sector than within the nonagricultural sector as a whole. . . .

---

[1] India (1950, 1955–1956), Ceylon (1952–1953), Northern Rhodesia (1946), Southern Rhodesia (1946), Kenya (1949), Mexico (1950, 1957), Colombia (1953), El Salvador (1946), Guatemala (1947–1948), Barbados (1951–1952), Puerto Rico (1953), Italy (1948), Great Britain (1951–1952), West Germany (1950), Netherlands (1950), Denmark (1952), Sweden (1948), and United States (1950).

(c) It follows from (a) and (b) that the distribution of income within the non-Agricultural is much more unequal in the underdeveloped countries than the developed countries.

(d) The limited sample of long-term records shows that the inequality in the size distribution of income in the developed countries has narrowed over time. . . .

(e) The pattern of the size distribution of income characterizing underdeveloped countries today is not too different from that observed in the presently developed countries in the 1920's and 1930's, or the beginning of the century—before the recent trend towards narrower inequality.

However, in regard to the two questions posed in the beginning of the study, he admits:

> But with the data at hand, we could not distinguish the effects of changes in the production system from those of modifications or distortions in the social structure that are necessary related to the former.
>
> Clearly, in evaluating the effects of the size distribution of income on economic growth, the knowledge of quantitative characteristics of the distribution itself is just beginning.

With these words, Kuznets set the stage for a lot of people to research the inverted U-shaped hypothesis (see figure 10.1). Many studies followed; more were empirical than theoretical. Some of the studies lend support to the inverted U-shaped hypothesis; other ones shed doubt on it. Cross-country empirical studies tend to support the hypothesis; one-country longitudinal studies tend not to find any evidence to support it. Cross-country empirical models that use the Gini coefficient as a measure of inequality tend not to support the hypothesis; however, those cross-country models that use the ratio of income shares of the top income groups to the lower income groups tend to support it. Theoretical models based on two sectors—that is, urban/rural or modern/traditional—tend to support the hypothesis. We will begin by looking at a sample of these kinds of models.

Two-Sector Models of the Inverted U-Shaped Hypothesis

In these kinds of models the economy starts out with one sector, the traditional sector. This makes sense if one thinks of very underdeveloped economies

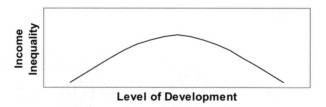

Level of Development

Figure 10.1. Kuznets Inverted U-Shaped Hypothesis

where the population hunts meat and gathers nuts, berries, and roots for food. In such an economy everyone is uniformly poor. In the next stage of development, animal husbandry is introduced as a technological improvement over hunting. Such societies are dependent on grazing land fostering a nomadic tribal lifestyle. Differences in wealth begin to appear as the herds of some members of the tribe grow larger than others. Eventually, crop cultivation is introduced, and the differences in the landholdings of some further aggravate the income distribution, but the differences are not too extreme until large plantations begin to appear, creating a landed aristocracy.

At some later point in time a modern sector of economic activity is introduced. The goods produced in the modern sector may be manufactures or some goods intended for foreign markets. When these goods command higher prices than those in the traditional sector, they yield a marginal revenue product of labor curve that is higher and steeper than that in the traditional sector. Labor in the traditional sector seeks employment in the modern sector with the expectation of higher wages. Hence there is a flow of labor out of the traditional sector into the modern sector (see Harris and Todaro [11] and Salvatore [18] for a more elegant and detailed model of the migration from the traditional to the modern sector).

For a while the wage rate in the modern sector will remain higher than that in the traditional sector but will decrease as more and more people migrate to it. This wage differential between the two sectors will create income inequality between the sectors. However, as people leave the traditional sector, the wage in that sector will rise until the marginal revenue product of labor curves for the two sectors cross (see figure 10.2). At that point, migration will stop, since there is no more expectation of a higher wage in the modern sector, and the income distribution will be more even. While this logic seems plausible, it suffers from rigor. Mathematically sophisticated readers may wish to look at the analysis of "modern sector enlargement growth" given by Gary S. Fields [7, at p. 342] of Cornell University.

Fields also examines the welfare implications of different types of dualistic economic development, of which modern sector enlargement is only one model. He also analyzes "traditional sector impoverishment" and "modern

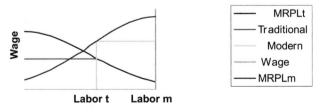

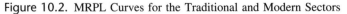

Figure 10.2. MRPL Curves for the Traditional and Modern Sectors

sector enrichment." He focuses on the important problem of what happens to the poor, in absolute terms. Another mathematically oriented paper that restricts the economy to two goods and two sectors is given by Campano and Salvatore [4].

Empirical Studies on the Inverted U-Shaped Hypothesis

Kuznets's empirical work on income distribution was a call-to-arms to collect more and better data on income distribution, especially for the developing countries. International institutions were concerned with the massive poverty found in the developing countries, and it was important to evaluate how effective the development aid flowing to the developing countries would be in addressing absolute poverty.

The World Bank responded by compiling whatever household sample surveys were available and standardizing the income distributions by deciles of population (these were published in Jain [12]). In the mid-1970s, Simon Goldberg, the director of the United Nations Statistical Office, initiated a household sample survey program designed to train statistical offices in developing countries to conduct household sample surveys with a consistent definition of income so that they could be compared internationally.

The data in Jain became the source data of income distribution for a long period of time and was used by many researchers. Perhaps the most influential study based on this data was the one done by Montek S. Ahluwalia [1] at the World Bank. Ahluwalia used the following cross-country model to test the Kuznets hypothesis:

$$1.\ Top_{20} = a_1 + b_1 \log_{10}(Y/P) + c_1 [\log_{10}(Y/P)]^2$$
$$2.\ Middle_{40} = a_2 + b_2 \log_{10}(Y/P) + c_2 [\log_{10}(Y/P)]^2$$
$$3.\ Lowest_{60} = a_3 + b_3 \log_{10}(Y/P) + c_3 [\log_{10}(Y/P)]^2$$
$$4.\ Lowest_{40} = a_4 + b_4 \log_{10}(Y/P) + c_4 [\log_{10}(Y/P)]^2$$
$$5.\ Lowest_{20} = a_5 + b_5 \log_{10}(Y/P) + b_5 [\log_{10}(Y/P)]^2$$

The left-hand side of each of the above equations was the share of total income flowing to each respective group. The explanatory variable (Y/P) was gross national product per capita expressed on constant U.S. dollars based on the period 1965–1971. He used per capita GNP as a rough proxy for the level of development but was well aware of the limitations of this choice:

> The true relationship between inequality and development must be fairly complex, reflecting the impact of a number of processes of structural change occurring with development. Such a complex relationship obviously cannot be "reduced" into a single explanatory variable. Per capita GNP is a useful summary measure of the level of development in the sense that it is correlated with most processes occurring with development, and as such, it may

capture the net effect of these processes as observed in the cross-country experience. [1, at p. 313]

He also adds in a footnote that the per capita GNP data did not take into account purchasing power parity, and comparisons with developed countries would probably understate the GNP in developing countries.

The above equations describe parabolas when $log_{10}(Y/P)$ is the explanatory variable. The Kuznets inverted U-shaped hypothesis would be supported by the estimation if equation 1 were concave *downward* and the others were concave *upward*. This is exactly the result that Ahluwalia got, but while the t-tests for each of the parameters were sufficiently high to accept the model, the coefficients of determination were weak unless a dummy variable was introduced for the socialist countries included in the sample. It appeared that the model could be used to project income distributions (see Ahluwalia, Carter, and Chenery [2]) for countries that were included in the sample and hence project levels of poverty under different scenarios of GNP growth, population growth, and income distribution change. This would be an important tool for developing country policy formation.

Ashwani Saith [17] reworked the equations estimated by Ahluwalia using the data by Jain [12]. He found that Ahluwalia's estimation of the inverted U-curve was considerably weakened when more restricted samples of countries were introduced. He concluded that "the cross-country U-Hypothesis is more of a hindrance than an aid to our comprehension of the relationship between economic growth and income distribution." This criticism dealt a serious blow to researchers who were convinced of the inverted U-hypothesis and who were reassured by Ahluwalia's estimation.

Many of Saith's criticisms were rebuked by Campano and Salvatore [3], who also reestimated Ahluwalia's equations, but this time using a different and expanded data set (see appendix I). The income shares flowing to the deciles of households were estimated from household sample survey data collected by the United Nations Statistical Office, the International Labor Office, country statistical offices, and other credible sources. Rigorous fitting of the income distribution models presented in chapter 5 provided the decile distributions used. The results indicated strong support for the inverted U-shaped hypothesis.

On the other hand, Fields [8], using a new World Bank data set, could only find "very tenuous empirical support" for the link between economic growth and the distribution of benefits received. Deininger and Squire [5] of the World Bank also found little support for the Kuznets hypothesis using what they viewed as the highest-quality cross-country data yet available. Randolph and Lott [16] did find support for the inverted U-shaped hypothesis by taking data that others used to show that there was little support for it. In their study they found statistical (econometric) problems with the equation specification and variable selection of previous studies. With these corrected, the support for the inverted U-shaped hypothesis was forthcoming.

These studies are a sample of all the empirical studies on the Kuznets hypothesis. Until more cross-country and time series data are available, the hypothesis will remain an open debate. However, recent changes in income distribution in the former socialist countries of Eastern Europe and in China may offer a clue on the direction of the debate in the future.

The Asian Experience

Among the market economies, Japan stands out as having one of the most even income distributions. Other countries in the Pacific Basin have adopted the Japanese model of development and have had similar improvement in their income distributions. What distinguishes this model of development is a combination of export orientation as proposed in the *neoliberal view* and attention to egalitarian social policies as proposed in the *redistribution view* defined by Galbraith [10]. It appears that both are necessary, as Wong and Arief [19] suggest in explaining income distribution in Southeast Asia.

For example, the Philippines, which has one of the lowest illiteracy rates among developing countries, 10% as compared to 22% for East Asia[2] in general, and a well-developed health-care system, has a rather skewed income distribution. Wong and Arief point out that the Philippines, along with Thailand, is still in the transition from an import-substitution to an export-promotion orientation. They argue that the high growth found in South Korea, Hong Kong, and Singapore is a result of an export orientation with a specialty in manufactures. Natural resource endowments, or the lack of, are not necessarily correlated with equitable growth.

They point out that cultural traditions, such as Confucianism, may be a contributing factor to more equitable growth. Even the legacy of being a former colony had some beneficial aspects in that colonialism "left behind some viable physical infrastructure and a modern administrative system, on the basis of which the national governments built up their respective development programmes." Their observation was that these economies with the higher per capita incomes or at the later stages of economic development tended to have a lower income inequality.

10.2 Projecting Income Shares Based on Per Capita GDP

In this section we will demonstrate how one can simulate the long-term prospect for income distribution and poverty for a developing country by using

---

[2]World Bank, *Social Indicators of Development 1995*, Baltimore, Md., Johns Hopkins University Press, 1995.

another estimation of the model proposed by Ahluwalia, Carter, and Chenery [2]. The difference in the estimation is that the following equations were estimated on a much larger data bank of decile data (see appendix I) using per capita GDP in 1975 U.S. constant dollars. Another difference is that natural logarithms were used, and the dummy variable for socialist countries was omitted.

1. $T_{20} = -6.55 + 20.26[\ln Y/P] - 1.68[\ln Y/P]^2$
2. $M_{40} = 60.29 - 10.08[\ln Y/P] + 0.90[\ln Y/P]^2$
3. $B_{60} = 79.47 - 17.07[\ln Y/P] + 1.36[\ln Y/P]^2$
4. $B_{40} = 46.75 - 10.34[\ln Y/P] + 0.79[\ln Y/P]^2$
5. $B_{20} = 18.97 - 4.17[\ln Y/P] + 0.30[\ln Y/P]^2$

If we adopt the convention that the lowest quintile will correspond to Q_1 and the highest will correspond to Q_5, then:

$$Q_5 = T_{20},$$
$$Q_1 = B_{20},$$
$$Q_2 = B_{40} - Q_1,$$
$$Q_3 = B_{60} - B_{40},$$
$$Q_4 = M_{40} - Q_3,$$
$$\textit{Note: } M_{40} = Q_4 + Q_3.$$

One country included in the sample to estimate the above equations was the Dominican Republic. The sample survey used was one that was conducted in 1977, and the quintile shares of GDP are given by:

$Q_1 = 4.53$, $Q_2 = 8.23$, $Q_3 = 12.09$, $Q_4 = 18.64$, and $Q_5 = 56.51$.

The population was 5.302 million people, and GDP in constant 1975 U.S. million dollars was \$2,529.054. Hence per capita GDP was \$477 (1975 constant U.S. dollars). Each quintile had a population of $5.302/5 = 1.0604$ million people, and the bottom 20% had an estimated $.0453 \times 2,529.054 = \$114.57$ million of the total GDP. Hence, the per capita income of the lowest quintile was about \$108. A similar computation indicates that the per capita income of the top 20% was about \$1,348. The United Nations (1996 revision)[3] medium variant projection of the population for the year 2005 is 9.123 million people. The long-term (1970–1997) trend growth rate of the Dominican Republic is about 3.5%. If we estimate potential GDP for the year 2005 based on that growth rate from 1977, we get \$5,786 (constant 1975 dollars), yielding a per capita income of about \$634. What can we expect the per capita income of the bottom and top 20% to be?

[3]United Nations, *World Population Prospects*, 1996 Revision, New York, United Nations, 1998.

We first adjust the constant coefficient in equations 1 and 5 above for the Dominican Republic. This is done by substituting the observation for the shares and GDP in 1977 and solving for a new constant coefficient. The natural logarithm of \$477 is 6.1675165, and its square is 38.03826. To adjust the equation for the top 20%, we substitute their share of GDP (56.51%) and the above logarithms into equation 1 and solve for the new constant. That is:

$$56.51 = X + 20.26(6.1675165) - 1.68(38.03826)$$
$$X = -4.54.$$

Hence, the constant coefficient for the Dominican Republic becomes -4.54. A similar computation for the bottom 20% changes the constant coefficient for equation 5 to 18.84. So our adjusted equations can be written as:

$$1'\, T_{20} = -4.54 + 20.26[\ln Y/P] - 1.68[\ln Y/P]^2$$
$$5'\, B_{20} = 18.84 - 4.17[\ln Y/P] + 0.3[\ln Y/P]^2.$$

Now substituting the estimated potential per capita GDP (\$634) for 2005 in the adjusted equations, we get the share of the bottom 20% as 4.42% and the share of the top 20% as 56.24%. With these shares of income, the bottom 20% will have a per capita income of $(.0442 \times \$5,686)/1.8246 = \$251.3$ (constant 1975 U.S. dollars), and the top 20% will have a per capita income of $(.5624 \times \$5,686)/1.8246 = \$1,752.6$ (constant 1975 U.S. dollars). This simulation indicates that while the income distribution slightly worsens over a 28-year period, both the top and bottom 20% have increased their per capita incomes in real terms. It also indicates the painfully long period of time it takes for developing countries to reach per capita incomes that the developed countries have enjoyed for decades.

Problems

The following problems make use of the estimated model 1 to 5 of the inverted U-shaped hypothesis.

1. One of the sample countries (country X) had the following quintile income distribution:

    $Q_1 = 5.29$, $Q_2 = 8.41$, $Q_3 = 11.92$, $Q_4 = 18.02$, and $Q_5 = 56.37$.

    GDP in 1981 was \$4,666.1 million (constant 1975 U.S. dollars). The population was 7.113 million people. The UN projection (1996 revision) for population in 2005 is 13.971 people. The average long-term growth rate of GDP is 1.6%. Estimate the per capita incomes of the top and bottom 20% for the year 2005 using the above growth rate of GDP.

2. Suppose the absolute poverty threshold were $500 per person (constant 1975 U.S. dollars). At what growth rate would the country have to grow in order to have all people above that threshold in 2005 if there were no income redistribution except for the changes resulting from the inverted U-shaped model?

3. Estimate the per capita income for the middle 40% for country X in 2005.

4. Find the level of per capita income when equality changes direction for each of the equations 1 to 5.

5. Estimate the quintile distribution for country X in 2005.

References

1. Ahluwalia, Montek S., *Inequality, Poverty and Development*, Journal of Development Economics, Vol. 3, 1976, pp. 307–342.

2. Ahluwalia, Montek S., Nicholas G. Carter, and Hollis B. Chenery, *Growth and Poverty in Developing Countries*, Journal of Development Economics, Vol. 6, 1979, pp. 1–79.

3. Campano, Fred and Dominick Salvatore, *Economic Development, Income Inequality, and Kuznets' U-Shaped Hypothesis*, Journal of Policy Modeling, June 1988, pp. 265–280.

4. Campano, Fred and Dominick Salvatore, *A Two-Sector Model, Two-Goods Model of Growth and Migration, and the Gini Coefficient*, in Franz Haslinger and Oliver Stonner-Venlatarama, eds., *Aspects of Income Distribution*, Marburg, Metropolis Verlag, 1998.

5. Deininger, Klaus and Lyn Squire, *New Ways of Looking at Old issues: Inequality and Growth*, Journal of Development Economics, Vol. 57, 1998, pp. 259–287.

6. Fields, Gary S., *Who Benefits from Economic Development? A Re-examination of Brazilian Growth in the 1960s*, American Economic Review, September 1977, pp. 570–582.

7. Fields, Gary S., *A Welfare Economic Approach to Growth and Distribution in the Dual Economy*, Quarterly Journal of Economics, August 1979, pp. 325–353.

8. Fields, Gary S., *Changes in Poverty and Inequality in Developing Countries*, World Bank Research Observer, Vol. 4, No. 2, 1989, pp. 167–185.

9. Forbes, Kristin, *A Reassessment of the Relationship between Inequality and Growth*, American Economic Review, September 2000, pp. 869–887.

10. Galbraith, James K., *A Perfect Crime: Inequality in the Age of Globalization*, Daedalus, Winter 2002, pp. 11–25.

11. Harris, J. R. and M. P. Todaro, *Migration, Unemployment and Development: A Two-sector Analysis*, American Economic Review, Vol. 60, No. 1, 1970, pp. 126–142.

12. Jain, S. *Size Distribution of Income: A Compilation of Data*, World Bank, Washington, D.C., 1975.

13. Kuznets, S., *Economic Growth and Income Inequality*, American Economic Review, March 1955, pp. 1–28.

14. Kuznets, S., *Quantitative Aspects of the Economic Growth of Nations: VIII. Distribution of Income by Size*, Economic Development and Cultural Change, Vol. 11, pt. 2, 1963, pp. 1–80.
15. Papanek, G. F. and O. Kyn, *The Effect on Income Distribution of Development, the Growth Rate and Economic Strategy*, Journal of Development Economics, Vol. 23, 1986, pp. 55–65.
16. Randolph, Susan M. and William F. Lott, *Can the Kuznets Effect be Relied on to Induce Equalizing Growth?*, World Development, Vol. 21, No. 5, 1993, pp. 829–840.
17. Saith, Ashwani, *Development and Distribution—A Critique of the Cross-Country U-Hypothesis*, Journal of Development Economics, Vol. 13, 1983, pp. 367–382.
18. Salvatore, D., *Internal Migration, Urbanization, and Economic Development*, in D.Salvatore, ed. *World Population Trends and Their Impact on Economic Development*, Westport, Conn., Greenwood Press, 1988.
19. Wong, John and Sritua Arief, *An Overview of Income Distribution in South Korea, Hong Kong, Indonesia, Malaysia, The Philippines, Singapore and Thailand*, South East Asian Economic Review, Vol. 5, No. 1, 1984, pp. 1–66.

11

Growth and Poverty in a Globalizing World

The past two decades have witnessed an increasingly rapid tendency toward globalization in the world economy, and this has significantly affected the rate of economic growth and poverty around the world. A great deal of controversy exists, however, on whether globalization has resulted in increased or reduced world inequalities and poverty. This chapter begins with an analysis of the process of globalization in production and labor markets during the past two decades and then proceeds to examine how globalization has affected economic growth and poverty around the world.

11.1 Globalization in Production and in Labor Markets

There is a strong trend toward globalization in production and labor markets in the world today, and this increases the efficiency, competitiveness, and growth of firms and nations that take advantage of this trend. Global corporations play a crucial role in the process of globalization. These are companies that are run by an international team of managers, that have research and production facilities in many countries, that use parts and components from the cheapest sources around the world, and that sell their products, finance their operations, and are owned by stockholders throughout the world.

More and more corporations operate today on the belief that their very survival requires them to be one of a handful of global corporations in their sector. This is true in the automobile industry, steel, aircrafts, computers, telecommunications, consumer electronics, chemicals, drugs, and many other products. Nestlé, the largest Swiss company and the world's second-largest food company, has production facilities in fifty-nine countries and America's Gillette in twenty-two. Ford has component factories in twenty-six different industrial sites around the world and assembly plants in six countries and employs more people abroad (181,000) than in the United States (169,000).

One important form of globalization in production is outsourcing, or the foreign "sourcing" of inputs. There is practically no major product today that does not have some foreign inputs. Foreign sourcing is often not a matter of choice for corporations to earn higher profits but simply a requirement for them to remain competitive. Firms that do not look abroad for cheaper inputs face loss of competitiveness in world markets and even in the domestic market.

This is the reason that $625 of the $860 total cost of producing an IBM PC was incurred for parts and components manufactured by IBM outside the United States or purchased from foreign producers during the mid-1980s. Such low-cost offshore purchase of inputs is likely to continue to expand rapidly in the future and is being fostered by joint ventures, licensing arrangements, and other nonequity collaborative arrangements. Indeed, this represents one of the most dynamic aspects of the global business environment of today.

Foreign sourcing can be regarded as manufacturing's new *international* economies of scale in today's global economy. Just as companies were forced to rationalize operations within each country in the 1980s, they now face the challenge of integrating their operations for their entire system of manufacturing around the world to take advantage of the new international economies of scale. What is important is for the firm to focus on those components that are indispensable to the company's competitive position over subsequent product generations and "outsource" all the rest from outside suppliers in order to have a distinctive production advantage.

Globalization in production has proceeded so far that it is now difficult to determine the nationality of many products. For example, should a Honda Accord produced in Ohio be considered American? What about a Chrysler minivan produced in Canada, especially now that Chrysler has been acquired by Daimler-Benz (Mercedes)? Is a Kentucky Toyota or Mazda that uses nearly 50% of imported Japanese parts American? It is clearly becoming more and more difficult to define what is American, and opinions differ widely. One could legitimately even ask if this question is relevant in a world growing more and more interdependent and globalized. Today, the ideal corporation is strongly decentralized to allow local units to develop products that fit into local cultures, and yet it is very centralized at its core to coordinate activities around the globe.

Even more dramatic than globalization in production has been the globalization of labor markets around the world. Work that was previously done in the United States and other industrial countries is now often done much more cheaply in developing countries. This is the case not only for low-skilled assembly-line jobs but also for jobs requiring high computer and engineering skills. Most Americans have only now come to fully realize that there is a truly competitive labor force in the world today, willing and able to do their job at a much lower cost. If anything, this trend is likely to accelerate in the future.

Even service industries are not immune to global job competition. For example, more than 3,500 workers on the island of Jamaica are connected to the United States by satellite dishes to make airline reservations, process tickets, answer calls to toll-free numbers, and do data entry for U.S. airlines at a much lower cost than could be done in the United States. Nor are highly skilled and professional people spared from global competition. A few years ago, Texas Instruments set up an impressive software programming operation in Bangalore, a city of 4 million people in southern India. Other American multinationals soon followed. Motorola, IBM, AT&T, and many other high-tech firms are now doing even a great deal of basic research abroad. In 2004, IBM indicated that it was going to shift about 7,500 hi-tech jobs abroad to lower costs.

Workers in advanced countries are beginning to raise strong objections to the transfer of skilled jobs abroad. All advanced countries are outsourcing more and more of their work to emerging markets in order to bring or keep costs down and remain internationally competitive. In the future, more and more work will simply be done in emerging markets best equipped to do the job most economically. If governments in advanced nations tried to restrict the flow of work abroad to protect domestic jobs their firms would risk losing, international competitiveness may end up having to move all of their operations abroad.

Globalization in production and labor markets is important and inevitable—important because it increases efficiency; inevitable because international competition requires it. Besides the well-known static gains from specialization in production and trade, globalization leads to even more important dynamic gains from extending the scale of operation to the entire world and from leading to the more efficient utilization of capital and technology of domestic resources at home and abroad. Globalization is inevitable because firms must outsource parts and components from wherever in the world they are made better or cheaper, and they must invest their capital and technology wherever they are more productive. Otherwise, competitors would do so, and the firm would lose its markets and might even be forced to shut down. For the same reason, firms must outsource labor services or employ labor offshore, where it is cheaper or more convenient.

The terrorist attack of September 11, 2001, and subsequent attacks sharply reduced travel, trade, and investment in the weeks following these tragedies. Although conditions have now returned to near normality, the cost of travel, transportation, and communications has risen in order to pay for increased controls and protection. This is like the imposition of a tariff or tax on international transactions and tends to slow down the process of globalization without, however, bringing it to a halt.

Globalization, Economic Growth, and Development

Growth is the most important economic goal of countries today. The best available measure of growth in standards of living that will also allow comparisons across countries is in terms of purchasing power parity (PPP) per capita incomes. Since we are interested in examining the effect of globalization on growth and development, we will compare the growth of real PPP per capita incomes in various countries and regions in the period 1980–2000, which is usually taken as the most recent period of rapid globalization, with the 1960–1980 preglobalization period. Of course, the rate of growth and development of a nation depends not only on globalization but also on many other domestic factors, such as political stability, improvements in education and labor skills, the rate of investment and absorption of new technology, the rate of population growth, and so on. But globalization is certainly a crucial ingredient to growth.

For example, no one forced China to open up to the world economy, but without such an opening, China would not have received the huge inflows of capital and technology, and it would not have been able to increase its exports so dramatically, and thus it would not have been able to achieve its spectacular rates of growth during the past decade. A possibly strong positive correlation between globalization and growth does not, of course, establish causality, but it would refute the assertion on the part of antiglobal groups that globalization has caused increased inequalities between advanced and developing countries during the past two decades.

Table 11.1 gives the weighted yearly average real PPP (with base 1993) per capita income in various regions and countries of the world in the 1960–1980 period and in the 1980–2000 period. From the table we see that Asia, except East Asia, did well during the 1960–1980 period and spectacularly well (especially China) during the 1980–2000 period. The Middle East and North Africa did well during the first period but very badly during the second period because of political turmoil and wars. Sub-Saharan Africa did not do well during the first period and actually became poorer during the second because of political instability, wars, droughts, and AIDS (acquired immuno deficiency syndrome). Latin America did well during the first period, but per capita incomes were practically stagnant during the second period, so that the 1980–2000 period can be considered lost decades as far as economic development is concerned because of political and economic crises.

The developing world as a whole did reasonably well during the first period and even better during the second. Eastern Europe did very well during the first period but suffered a significant decline in average per capita incomes during the second period as a result of the economic collapse associated with the fall of communism and the required economic restructuring that followed it. Overall, only Asia grew faster than industrialized countries and sharply reduced

Table 11.1 Weighted Yearly Average Real PPP Per Capita Income
Percentage Growth in Various Regions, 1960–1980 and 1980–2000

Region	1960–1980	1980–2000
East Asia	2.85	6.12
South Asia	0.55	3.00
Asia	1.98	4.86
China and India	1.74	5.75
Middle East & North Africa	3.21	0.15
Sub-Saharan Africa	1.29	−0.58
Latin America	3.13	0.08
Developing World	2.12	3.11
Developing World, excl.		
China & India	2.51	0.69
Eastern Europe	4.03	−1.88
Nonindustrialized World	2.32	2.84
Industrialized World	3.27	1.55
World	2.50	2.65

Sources: World Bank, *Globalization, Growth and Poverty: Building an Inclusive World Economy*, New York, Oxford University Press, 2002; Bhalla, Surjit S., *Imagine There's No Country*, Washington, Institute for International Economics, 2002.

inequalities vis-à-vis industrialized countries as a group during the 1980–2000 period. Latin America, the Middle East, and North Africa did poorly, and so inequalities with respect to industrialized countries increased. Sub-Saharan Africa and Eastern Europe actually became poorer in an absolute sense during the second period with respect to the first, and so they fell further behind industrialized countries and developing Asia.

Table 11.2 shows more directly the correlation between globalization and growth. It shows that the growth of real per capita PPP GDP increased sharply in each decade from 1960 to 2000 for the developing countries that globalized (i.e., those in which the ratio of trade to GDP increased) and far exceeded the average growth of rich countries and that of nonglobarizers during the past two decades. The growth of rich countries was very high and much higher than for globalizers and nonglobalizers during the decade of the 1960s, but it declined in each subsequent decade. The growth of nonglobalizers increased from the

Table 11.2 Weighted Yearly Average Real PPP Per Capita
Income Growth in Rich Countries, Globalizers and
Nonglobalizers, 1960s, 1970s, 1980s, and 1990s

Group of Countries	1960s	1970s	1980s	1990s
Rich Countries	4.7	3.1	2.3	2.2
Globalizers	1.4	2.9	3.5	5.0
Nonglobalizers	2.4	3.3	0.8	1.4

Source: Dollar, David and Aron Kraay, *Growth Is Good for the Poor*, Policy Research Working Paper 2587, Washington, World Bank, 2001.

decade of the 1960s to the decade of the 1970s, but then it declined sharply during the 1980s and was very low during the 1990s. It seems that growth can be rapid without liberalization and globalization at the beginning of the growth process, but as the nation develops, economic efficiency associated with liberalization and globalization becomes increasingly important.

Although there is no perfect correspondence between nonglobalizers and the poorest countries in the world, most nonglobalizers do include most of the poorest countries in the world. Thus, inequalities in per capita incomes and standards of living did increase between nonglobalizers, on the one hand, and globalizers and rich countries, on the other. But the fault for this increased inequality cannot be attributed to globalization, as such. Indeed, it was the globalizers that grew fast, while the nonglobalizers stagnated or regressed. Thus, the only criticism that can be levied against globalization, as a process, is that it did not permit the poorest countries in the world to also participate in the tremendous benefits in terms of economic efficiency and growth in living standards that globalization made possible. This is a far cry from globalization being itself the cause of the increased inequalities between the rich and the globalizing developing countries and the poorest developing nations during the past two decades, as claimed by the opponents of globalization.

11.2 Globalization and Poverty

Another important question that needs to be answered is what effect globalization has had on actual world poverty at the country level and at the individual level. Depending on how we choose to measure relative poverty, however, we get dramatically different results.

One way to measure the evolution of relative poverty is to measure the change in the number of times that the income per capita in the richest country (the United States, if we exclude such a small country as Luxembourg) exceeds the income per capita in the world's poorest country, in the tenth poorest country, or in the 20 poorest countries as compared with the 20 richest countries in the world over time. Based on this measure, the United Nations [18], the World Bank [19], and several eminent economists, such as Pritchett [12] and Stiglitz [17], have asserted that globalization caused or resulted in increased income inequalities and poverty in the poorest developing countries over the past decades.

The data presented in table 11.3 shed light on this position. The second column of the table shows that the ratio of real PPP per capita income in the United States relative to the poorest country (Lesotho) was 48.3 in 1960, 47.1 (Lesotho) in 1970, 47.4 (Tanzania) in 1980, 51.6 (Tanzania) in 1990, and 73.3 (Sierra Leone) in 2000. Thus, according to this measure, world income inequalities have indeed increased significantly from 1960 to 2000. To avoid

Table 11.3 Ratio of Real PPP Per Capita Income in Rich
and Poor Countries, 1960–2000

Year	In U.S. Relative to Poorest Country	In U.S. Relative to 10th Poorest Country	In the 20 Richest Countries Relative to the 20 Poorest Countries
1960	48.3	27.6	23.0
1970	47.1	31.0	26.2
1980	47.4	31.3	25.7
1990	51.6	32.5	30.8
2000	73.3	44.6	36.3

Sources: World Bank, *Globalization, Growth and Poverty: Building an Inclusive World Economy*, New York, Oxford University Press, 2002; Bhalla, Surjit S., *Imagine There's No Country*, Washington, Institute for International Economics, 2002.

the problem of outliers, the third column of table 11.3 shows that the ratio of real per capita PPP income in the United States relative to the tenth poorest country (Guinea-Bissau) was 27.6 in 1960, 31.0 (Nigeria) in 1970, 31.3 (Bhutan) in 1980, 32.5 (Burundi) in 1990, and 44.6 (Zambia) in 2000. Thus, again inequalities seem to have increased. Finally, the same conclusion can be reached from the last column of table 11.3 when inequalities are measured as the ratio of the top 20 countries to the bottom 20 countries.

A different and more direct method of measuring changes in poverty around the world is to measure the change in the number of poor *people*. There are two ways of doing this: One utilizes national accounts data, and the other uses data from national surveys. Table 11.4 gives the number of people and the proportion of the total population who lived on less than $1.50 per day at 1993 prices (which is equivalent to the $1.00 per day at 1985 prices used by the World Bank as a measure of poverty in terms of PPP) in various regions and countries of the world in 1960, 1970, 1980, 1990, and 2000 using national accounts data, as presented by Bhalla [3] from World Bank data [20]. The top portion of table 11.4 shows that the number of poor people increased from 1.13 billion in 1960 to 1.48 billion in 1980, but then it declined to 1.06 billion in 1990 and 0.68 billion in 2000. As a percentage of the total population of developing countries, the number of poor people declined from 52.5 in 1960 to 43.5 in 1980 and 13.1 in 2000. Thus, according to this data, there was a dramatic decline in the number and in the proportion of poor people during the most recent period of rapid globalization from 1980 to 2000.

Of the reduction in the number of the world's poor of 832 million between 1980 and 2000 shown in table 11.4, 520 million was in China, 115 million was in India, and 197 million in other developing countries. Only in Sub-Saharan Africa did the number of poor increase significantly during the past two decades. For the most part, these were also the countries that failed to globalize and experienced wars, political instability, droughts, and AIDS. Also using national accounts data, Sala-i-Martin [13], however, estimates that the number

Table 11.4 World Poverty: Percentage and Number of People Living on Less Than $1.50 per Day, 1960–2000

Region	Number of Poor People				
	1960	1970	1980	1990	2000
East Asia	729	833	955	521	114
South Asia	209	229	310	207	105
Sub-Saharan Africa	118	150	188	279	362
Middle East & North Africa	32	23	10	16	29
Latin America	35	27	13	23	27
Eastern Europe	29	12	7	0	0
Developing World	1,131	1,262	1,479	1,056	647
Region	Ratio of Poor People				
East Asia	77.5	71.1	67.2	31.3	6.0
South Asia	37.2	32.1	34.4	18.5	7.8
Sub-Saharan Africa	53.2	52.2	49.9	55.3	54.8
Middle East & North Africa	24.3	13.4	4.3	5.2	7.8
Latin America	16.0	9.4	3.6	5.3	5.2
Eastern Europe	9.2	3.3	1.7	0	0
Developing World	52.5	46.4	43.5	25.4	13.1

Sources: World Bank, *Globalization, Growth and Poverty: Building an Inclusive World Economy*, New York, Oxford University Press, 2002; Bhalla, Surjit S., *Imagine There's No Country*, Washington, Institute for International Economics, 2002.

of poor were fewer than indicated in table 11.4 to begin with but declined by less from 1980 to 1998.

Chen and Ravallion [4] of the World Bank criticize these poverty data based on national accounts as grossly biased. Using instead data from nationally representative household surveys, the World Bank [21] estimated that the number of people living in poverty declined from 33% of world population in 1981 (about 1.5 billion people) to 18% in 2001 (about 1.1 billion people), or by 400 million (as compared with a decline from 43.5 to 13.1% or by over 800 million shown in table 11.4), but that almost all of this reduction occurred in China, thus leaving world poverty practically unchanged outside China (and actually increasing in Sub-Saharan Africa).

Thus, we can arrive at the general conclusion that relative poverty seems to have increased around the world when measured by average national incomes across nations. Looking at individuals rather than nations as a whole, however, we find that the number of people who live in poverty (defined as those who live on less than $1 per day in terms of 1985 PPP) decreased significantly over the past two decades, but most of this decrease occurred in China.

Problems

1. Suppose you are the chief operating officer for a large European toy manufacturer. One of your products, radio-controlled cars, is in

Table 11.5 Processes to Produce 100 Cars per Hour

Process	Units of Capital	Units of Labor
I	1	10
II	2	8
III	3	6
IV	4	4
V	5	2

competition with similar cars produced in Asian, American, and other European firms. To be competitive in world markets, you must sell at a price of 30 euros per car. Table 11.5 shows five different processes available to produce 100 cars per hour, each process based on a different technology.

Assume that capital is mobile—that is, it can be moved anywhere in the world—and also assume that the rental price of one unit of capital is 30 euros per hour.

a. At present the firm is paying 12 euros an hour for labor. Which process would you select? How many units of labor would be employed? Compute the profit on 100 cars.

b. Suppose the domestic socioeconomic realities force you to raise the labor rate to 16 euros. Which process would you select? How many units of labor would be employed? Compute the profit on 100 cars.

c. Suppose you could move production of this product to an African country where the labor rate is 5 euros per hour. Which process would you select? Compute the profit on 100 cars.

2. Foreign direct investment (FDI) by large transnational corporations can be netted out for any particular country by subtracting the amount of outflows from the amount of inflows. Each year the *World Investment Report* (*WIR*) published by the United Nations gives detailed tables of these flows.

a. Obtain from the latest *WIR* the net FDI for the United States.

b. Does the flow of FDI from the developed countries to the developing countries indicate a serious loss of employment for the developed countries?

c. Does the trend in per capita FDI data indicate a worsening of the poverty situation in the developing countries?

References

1. Barro, Robert J. and Xavier Sala-i-Martin, *Economic Growth*, second edition, Cambridge, Mass., MIT Press, 2004.

2. Bhagwati, Jagdish, *In Defense of Globalization*, New York, Oxford University Press, 2004.
3. Bhalla, Surjit S., *Imagine There's No Country*, Washington, Institute for International Economics, 2002.
4. Chen, Shaohua and Martin Ravallion, *How Have the World's Poor Fared since 1980?* World Bank Research Observer, Vol. 19, No. 2, 2004, pp. 141–169.
5. Dollar, David and Aron Kraay, *Growth Is Good for the Poor*, Policy Research Working Paper 2587, Washington, World Bank, 2001.
6. Dollar, David and Aron Kraay, *Trade, Growth and Poverty*, Economic Journal, February, 2004, pp. 22–49.
7. Dunning, John H., ed., *Making Globalization Good*, New York, Oxford University Press, 2004.
8. Frankel, Jeffrey, *Globalization of the Economy*, NBER Working Paper 7858, August 2000.
9. Grilli, Enzo and Dominick Salvatore, *Economic Development*, Westport, Conn., Greenwood Press, 1994.
10. IMF, *World Economic Outlook*, Washington, IMF, April 2004.
11. McKibbin, Warwick and Dominick Salvatore, *The Global Economic Consequences of the Uruguay Round*, Open Economies Review, April 1995, pp. 111–129.
12. Pritchett, Lant, *Divergence, Big Time*, Journal of Economic Perspectives, No. 3, 1997, pp. 3–17.
13. Sala-i-Martin, Xavier, *The World Distribution of Income*, NBER Working Paper 8933, May 2002.
14. Salvatore, Dominick, *Protectionism and World Welfare*, New York, Cambridge University Press, 1993.
15. Salvatore, Dominick, *International Trade and Economic Development*, Institutions and Economic Development, Fall 2003, pp. 5–26.
16. Stern, Nicholas, *A Strategy for Development*, Washington, World Bank, 2002.
17. Stiglitz, Joseph, *Globalization and Its Discontents*, New York, 2002.
18. United Nations, *Human Development Report 2003*, New York, Oxford University Press, 2003.
19. World Bank, *World Development Report 2000/2001*, NewYork, Oxford University Press, 2001.
20. World Bank, *Globalization, Growth and Poverty: Building an Inclusive World Economy*, New York, Oxford University Press, 2003.
21. World Bank, *World Development Indicators*, Washington, World Bank, 2004.
22. World Commission on the Social Dimension of Globalization, *A Fair Globalization*, Geneva, ILO, 2004.

12

Redistribution of Income

If we start with the premise that society owes each individual a minimum living standard and that access to such basic needs as education, health care, adequate housing, drinkable water, and proper sewerage are rights of the individuals of society, then it is not hard to see that it is the government's responsibility to make adjustments when these things are lacking. From at least the time of the pharaohs, governments have intervened to redistribute output. Such efforts were necessary to avoid massive starvation and to placate the poorer populations of society, lest they rebel.

Whatever the intentions of the government, however, designing a public redistribution program poses a number of difficult problems, some purely technical, others political. Perhaps the biggest obstacle to governments' efforts to redistribute is the fear by those politically opposed that these efforts will lead to waste and consequently to a lower standard of living for all. The design of a public program therefore must start with realistic goals that incorporate a benefit-cost analysis and a projection of the future funding to sustain the program.

In this chapter we will address some of these issues and consider the case found in many countries where public expenditure on basic needs is not enough to elevate everyone above the poverty threshold.

12.1 Income Taxes and Public Expenditure

In the developed countries public expenditure redistributes income from the richer households to the poorer households. The extent of this redistribution depends on the public priorities of the country, and there is always considerable debate on these priorities. To get an idea of distributive impact of government expenditures at one point of time in the United States, we will refer to a study

Table 12.1 U.S. Income Shares, Tax Shares, and Expenditure Shares by Quintile of Households, 1970

Quintile	% Income	% Local Tax	% Local Expend.	% Fed. Tax	% Fed. Expend.
Poorest	3.51	7.06	16.64	5.29	14.00
Q_2	10.03	13.34	18.21	9.89	22.43
Q_3	17.32	19.05	19.24	17.34	20.72
Q_4	24.71	24.41	21.34	30.23	20.83
Richest	44.53	36.20	24.57	42.63	22.02

Source: Ruggles, Patricia and Michael O'Higgins, *The Distribution of Public Expenditure among Households in the United States*, Review of Income and Wealth, series 27, 1981, table 1.

done by Patricia Ruggles and Michael O'Higgens [5] that is based on data from the 1970 census. Table 12.1 is a summary of table 1 in their study.

In table 12.1 we see that the poorest quintile of households received 3.51% of the total household income. That is, 20% of the households received only 3.51% of the available household income. However, at the local level, while this group paid 7.06% of the local taxes, they received 16.64% of the benefits from local public expenditure. Furthermore, at the federal level, they contributed 5.29% of the federal tax revenue and received in return 14% of the benefits flowing to households from federal expenditure. Hence at the local level they had a $16.64 - 7.06 = 9.58\%$ net gain from public expenditure, and at the federal level, their net gain was 8.71%. On the other hand, the richest quintile had a net loss at the local level of 11.63% and a net loss at the federal level of 20.61%. This represents the redistribution of income through government taxation and expenditure.

Progressive Marginal Tax Rates and the Distribution of Taxes to Quintiles of Households

We will now take a more careful look at the mechanism of a progressive tax system and how the tax burden may be shifted because of income changes and tax credits. Consider first a tax rate schedule for households where husband and wife file a joint income tax return. This is a simplification since a household may consist of more income recipients who are liable for income taxes than just the primary husband and wife in the household. Table 12.2 contains the tax rate schedule.

To compute its tax, the household reduces its gross income from various sources with whatever tax deductions it has. This becomes the *taxable* income, and the tax rate schedule is used. For example, if a household has a taxable income of $60,000, then the income tax will be $6,780 + .275(60,000 - 45,200) = \$10,850$. This tax rate schedule is called progressive because higher-income households have a higher marginal tax rate.

Table 12.2 Income Tax Rate Schedule

Taxable Income ($)	Tax Computation (%)	Of Amount Over ($)
0–45,200	15	0
45,200–109,250	6,780 + 27.5	42,200
109,250–166,500	24,393.75 + 30.5	109,250
166,500–297,350	41,855.00 + 35.5	166,500
297,350+	88,306.75 + 39.1	297,350

Now let us simulate a macroeconomic situation in which the economy is expanding along its potential GDP path and the distribution of pretax income by quintile of household is given in table 12.3. For each of these quintiles the income tax is computed under the assumption that all households in each quintile have the mean pretax income and each will take a standard deduction of $6,650. This is another simplification, but it will help us see the changes in the tax distribution due to income changes, capital gains tax changes, and tax credits.

In this simulation, the lowest quintile will have about 3.6% of the pretax income and pay about 1.03% of the government revenue from income tax. The highest quintile will have about 49.7% of the pretax income and pay about 62.57% of the government revenue from income tax. Now let us simulate a macroeconomic situation where the economy is rapidly expanding and GDP is above potential. Assume that the income tax rate schedule has not changed for a period of 10 years and that at the end of 10 years the nominal incomes of the lowest quintile increase by 10%, while the nominal incomes of the highest quintile increase by 50% over the same period. Then the lowest quintile will have a mean income of $11,204.60, and the highest quintile will have a mean income of $212,431.50. Furthermore, assume that the other quintiles increase their mean incomes by 20%, 30%, and 40%, respectively, for the second, third, and fourth quintiles. The recomputed income taxes are shown in table 12.4.

We see in table 12.4 that the high growth of income for the highest quintile raised the marginal income tax rate for the average household in that group from 35.5% to 39.1%. The only other group whose marginal tax rises is the middle quintile, which moves from the 15% bracket to the 27.5% bracket. The

Table 12.3 Mean Income and Mean Taxes Paid by Quintiles of Households (Assume $6,650 Standard Deduction)

Quintile	Mean Pretax Income ($)	Taxable Income ($)	Income Tax ($)	% of Total Taxes Paid
Lowest	10,186	3,536	530.40	1.03
Q₂	25,331	18,681	2,802.15	5.44
Q₃	42,359	35,709	5,356.35	10.40
Q₄	65,727	59,077	10,596.18	20.56
Highest	141,621	134,971	32,238.66	62.57

Table 12.4 Mean Income and Mean Taxes Paid by Quintiles of Households Recomputed After Ten Years (Assume $6,650 Standard Deduction)

Quintile	Mean Pretax Income ($)	Taxable Income ($)	Income Tax ($)	% of Total Taxes Paid
Lowest	11,205	4,555	683.25	0.87
Q_2	30,397	23,747	3,562.05	4.53
Q_3	55,067	48,417	7,664.68	9.75
Q_4	92,018	85,368	17,826.20	22.67
Highest	212,432	205,782	55,800.11	70.96

government will collect more taxes, and if tax revenue exceeds government expenditure, there will be a budget surplus. In such a situation, there will be political pressure to decrease marginal tax rates for the highest quintile since they are paying more than 70% of the total tax revenue. Furthermore, the two highest quintiles together will be paying over 90% of the total income tax revenue.

The main point of this simulation exercise is to demonstrate how the marginal tax bracket will increase for those quintiles whose incomes are rising if no adjustment is made to the income marginal rates. During a period when the incomes of the upper quintiles are growing slower than the lower quintiles, then their share of the total tax will decrease if the tax rates are not adjusted. In this case the government could collect less taxes. A situation like this might arise if there is a stock market adjustment in a negative direction, upper quintile incomes decrease, and a recession sets in.

In most countries the recession will cause unemployment, but in developed countries because of built-in income stabilizers, the changes in lower quintile incomes are generally not as much affected as the changes in upper quintile incomes. Upper quintiles will take tax reductions because of their investment losses, and it is quite possible that the lower quintiles will end up paying a larger share of the total tax. A change in the capital gains tax, as was enacted in the United States in 2003, will lower the tax of the upper deciles. This is one way of returning surplus taxes collected when upper quintile marginal tax brackets have increased because of rising income. Another way would be to lower the marginal income tax rates.

Income credits given to lower quintiles, such as an earned income credit, benefit lower quintile wage earners by reducing their tax share. An earned income may give a refund to people even if they do not owe any income tax. To qualify for an earned income credit, there are usually a number of conditions, such as (1) main income is from employment, (2) household income is below an income threshold, (3) the household is working legally in the country. The legality requirement is one reason why countries with large illegal immigrant populations do not seem to make much progress in reducing poverty.

Income Mobility

While the quintile shares of the total tax revenue collected by the government may vary with macroeconomic fluctuations, the tax liability of any individual household or person can change substantially from one year to the next. If the number of wage earners in a household changes, then the household's marginal tax rate can be radically affected.

For example, if a household has been relying on two income earners, say, husband and wife, and suddenly one of the children of the household finishes school and works full-time, the household now has three wage earners, and the marginal income and consequently marginal income tax bracket can sharply change. Likewise, if an income earner in a household leaves the household and sets up a new household, both households can move to a lower quintile. There are many factors that can affect household income, including retirement, divorce, the economy, additional education, and age. In regard to age, life-cycle income generally increases until the mid-fifties and then decreases. All of these contribute to household income mobility and hence to changes in household tax liability.

In analyzing the changes in the tax burden of different quintiles over time, it is important to keep in mind that households do not necessarily remain in the same quintile over the period of time being studied. Some countries have more income mobility than others. In principle, income mobility should be based on human effort and marginal revenue product or the marginal contribution a person makes to society. The more static income mobility is in a country, the lower it is on the development scale. An interesting study on the extent of income mobility in the United States between the years 1975 to 1991 is given by Cox and Alm [4].

Public Expenditure Benefits

We start out with the idea that public spending should benefit the whole society even if it is earmarked for one segment of the society. For example, government spending on higher education for students coming from households in the lower quintiles of income benefits the country in general because over their lifetime these more educated citizens will be more productive than they might otherwise be if they did not have the opportunity to go to college.

However, the education benefit that is given to the lower quintile household will appear from an accounting point of view only to benefit the lower quintiles. Hence the analysis that follows neglects the positive externalities that flow to all quintiles when lower quintiles benefit from government expenditure. Of course, wasteful government expenditure does not benefit anyone, and hence some sort of benefit-cost analysis should be done by government agencies to decide on which expenditure items to implement or continue and which to reject or terminate.[1]

In developing countries, where resources are not only scare but precious, it is even more important to avoid wasteful government expenditure. The design of efficient public spending programs that target the poor can be tricky. For example, in the 1970s UNESCO came to the conclusion that if literacy is the most important educational objective, then a policy of expanding elementary education[2] in rural areas at the expense of higher education in urban areas is a much more efficient use of scare educational funding. Of course, it would be better to be able to do both, but in many developing countries, budgetary constraints force making compromises. The difficulty with such a policy is that there is at least a nine-year lag before the child who is taught to read and write is able to realize any income benefits from the education received. The hope here is that future generations of the family will be better off because of the opportunity to be literate.

Middle- and upper-class families will push for spending on higher education because they place a high value on it, and they want their children to have access to it. While most universities are based on competitive examinations and not on ability to pay, in developing countries it is mainly the children of middle and upper classes who finally go to university because their families made sure that they get the proper preparation for higher learning. The emphasis on primary education has long-term benefits for income distribution; however, expenditure on universities can have benefits that have a much shorter payback period but do not necessarily help income distribution. Designing an educational expenditure policy that is optimal, that is, to strike the proper balance between spending on primary and secondary education and spending on higher education, is not an easy task, especially because of the time lags involved.

Similar difficulties arise in public health expenditure. How do developing country health officials decide on how much of the health budget should be earmarked for primary health care in rural areas and how much for modern hospitals in the urban areas? In developed countries the debate centers around the amount the government should pay of a citizen's cost of access to health care. If we assume that the average person will use the medical care system as long as the marginal benefit received is greater than the marginal cost, then if the marginal cost is 0 (because the government pays), long lines will appear at medical facilities.

---

[1]See Salvatore, Dominick, *Microeconomics Theory and Applications*, fourth edition, New York, Oxford University Press, 2003, for a more complete discussion on benefit-cost analysis in government expenditure.

[2]This emphasis on elementary education was established to meet the goal of eliminating illiteracy by the year 2000.

The design of the appropriate health system for any particular country is also not an easy task, but the World Health Organization (WHO)[3] offers some advice:

> Better health is unquestionably the primary goal of a health system. But because health care can be catastrophically costly and the need for it unpredictable, mechanisms for sharing risk and providing financial protection are important. A second goal of health systems is therefore fairness in financial contribution. A third goal—responsiveness to people's expectations in regard to non-health matters—reflects the importance of respecting people's dignity, autonomy and the confidentiality of information. WHO has engaged in a major exercise to obtain and analyze data in order to assess how far health systems in WHO Member States are achieving these goals for which they should be accountable, and how efficiently they are using their resources in doing so.

Inefficient public spending has been observed by researchers at the World Bank (see Birdsall and James [1]). Their research indicates that all too often the major beneficiaries of public spending on universities are the middle- and upper-income groups and that building hospitals in urban areas mainly serves people in urban areas. This contributes to the massive rural to urban migration found in many developing countries. Schwartz and Ter-Minassian [7] of the International Monetary Fund sum up the problem of efficient public spending as one of a trade-off between "policies that enhance cost efficiency and those that do not, and between policies that benefit the poor and those that do not."

12.2 An Income Redistribution Scheme

Often public expenditure is not enough to meet the needs of the poor. In some countries a minimum income policy might be needed to bring the entire population above the subsistence level. For example, it might be desired to have a minimum income of $250 per person in a country to avoid abject poverty. If we assume that the transfers to the lower quintiles are from the incomes of the upper to *deciles* of income,[4] then we can roughly compute the amount of transfer necessary to meet the minimum income policy. If we let S_i $(i = 1, \ldots, 10)$ be the share of income of the ith decile, then it follows:

---

[3]World Health Organization, *The World Health Report 2000: Health Systems: Improving Performance*, Geneva, WHO, 2000, chapter 2.
[4]We divide the richest quintile into two deciles because the incomes in the top decile are often widely distributed within the decile. For example, in the upper decile of the United States there are people who have incomes around $100,000 and others who have incomes over $5 million. The range of income in the other deciles is not so great.

$$S_i \leq S_{i+1} \text{ for all } I \tag{1}$$

$$\sum S_i = 1 \tag{2}$$

Now let S_9^* and S_{10}^* be the adjusted shares of the ninth and tenth deciles after redistribution. Hence:

$$S_9^* \leq S_9 \text{ and } S_{10}^* \leq S_{10} \tag{3}$$

$$S_8 \leq S_9^* \leq S_{10}^*. \tag{4}$$

Next define S_a as the share of the total income that must be allocated to the deciles that need additional income to meet the minimum income requirements. Then by definition:

$$S_a = (S_9 - S_9^*) + (S_{10} - S_{10}^*). \tag{5}$$

However, equation (4) implies:

$$S_9^* = S_8 + x \text{ and } S_{10}^* = S_8 + mx, \tag{6}$$

where $x \geq 0$ and m is a constant of proportionality between S_9 and S_{10}. That is:

$$m = (S_{10} - S_8)/(S_9 - S_8). \tag{7}$$

From equation (5) we have:

$$S_9^* + S_{10}^* = S_9 + S_{10} - S_a \tag{8}$$

Substituting S_9^* and S_{10}^* from equation (6), we obtain:

$$S_8 + x + S_8 + mx = S_9 + S_{10} - S_a. \tag{9}$$

Solving for x yields:

$$x = (S_9 + S_{10} - S_a - 2S_8)/(1 + m).$$

Example 1

A country has a total GDP of \$52,804.8 million and a population of 122.802 million people. Therefore, its per capita income is \$430. Suppose it is decided by the government that the poverty line should be set at \$200, and an estimation of the redistribution of income from the top two deciles to the quintiles below poverty line should be made. The income distribution for the country is given by table 12.5.

From table 12.5 we can directly set S_{10} to 25.2, S_8 to 12.0, and since the share of Q_5 is 39.7, we can set S_9 to $39.7 - 25.2 = 14.5$. The bottom quintile is the only quintile below the poverty line. Hence we can compute:

$$S_a = \frac{.0245608(200 - 180.60)}{52.8048} = .00902354,$$

Table 12.5 Income Distribution for Country in Example 1

	% Share of GDP	Per Capita Income ($)
Richest Decile D_{10}	25.2	1,083.60
D_8	12.0	516.00
Richest Quintile Q_5	39.7	853.55
Q_4	22.2	477.30
Q_3	16.9	363.35
Q_2	12.9	277.35
Q_1	8.4	180.60

where $200 - 180.60 = \$19.40$ is the per capita increase needed in the fifth quintile to raise the average above the poverty line. This must be given to .0245608 billion ($.122802/5 = .024608$) people who belong to the fifth quintile. As a share of the total GDP in percent, it becomes .902354%. The new share of income for the fifth quintile will be $8.4\% + .902354\% = 9.302355\%$.

Next we compute the constant of proportionality m.

$$m = \frac{25.2 - 12}{14.5 - 12} = 5.28.$$

Also the richest quintile will have to reduce its share of the total GDP by .902354%, that is, $S_9^* + S_{10}^* = 39.7 - .902354 = 38.797646\%$. To see how this would be divided between the two upper deciles, we compute x:

$$x = \frac{38.797646 - 2(12)}{1 + 5.28} = 2.3563131.$$

It follows that:

$$S_9^* = 12 + 2.3563131 = 14.356313\% \text{ and}$$
$$S_{10}^* = 12 + (5.28 \times 2.3563131) = 24.441333\%.$$

This example shows how for a modest reduction of about .76% in the share of income flowing to the richest decile of population and an even smaller reduction of about .144% of the next richest decile, the bottom quintile of population can raise its average per capita income from $180.60 to $200.

Problems

1. Use tables 12.2 and 12.3 to simulate a macroeconomic situation in which GDP is growing below potential for 5 years and at the end of 5 years the lowest quintile has increased its average nominal household income by 10%, the second quintile by 7%, the third quintile by 6%, and the fourth by 3%, and the highest quintile suffers a decrease of 2%.

Assume the marginal tax rates do not change. Compute the share of total income taxes paid by each quintile. Does total tax revenue increase or decrease?

2. Would you expect income inequality to increase or decrease in the simulation exercise of problem 1?

3. Change the poverty line to $250 in Example 1.

References

1. Birdsall, Nancy and Estelle James, *Efficiency and Equity in Social Spending: How and Why Governments Misbehave*, in Michael Lipton and Jacques van der Gang, eds., *Including the Poor*, Washington, World Bank, 1993.
2. Campano, F. *Income Distribution in Africa*, in Dominick Salvatore, ed., *African Development Prospects/A Policy Modeling Approach*, New York, Taylor and Francis, 1989, p.79.
3. Congressional Budget Office, *Historical Effective Tax Rates, 1979–1997*, Washington, GPO, May 2001.
4. Cox, Michael W. and Richard Alm, *By Our Own Bootstrings: Economic Opportunity and the Dynamics of Income Distribution*, Dallas, Tex., Federal Reserve Bank of Dallas, 1995.
5. Ruggles, Patricia and Michael O'Higgins, *The Distribution of Public Expenditure among Households in the United States*, Review of Income and Wealth, Series 27, 1981, pp. 137–163.
6. Salvatore, Dominick, *Microeconomics: Theory and Applications*, 4th ed, New York, Oxford University Press, 2003, Chapter 18.
7. Schwartz, Gerd and Teresa Ter-Minassian, *The Distributional Effects of Public Expenditure: Update and Overview*, IMF Working Paper wp/95/84, Washington, International Monetary Fund, 1995.
8. United Nations Development Programme, *Human Development Report 2003*, New York, Oxford University Press, 2003.

13

Integrating Macroeconomic Models with Income Distribution Models

F inding a connection between the functional distribution of income and the personal distribution of income has been as elusive as it is important. Until recently (about 1996), it remained as one of the missing links in economic theory; however, thanks to contributions by Dagum [6] and Galbraith [7], there is optimism that a unifying theory will emerge before long. Dagum's contribution derives an income-generating function from the product of two marginal distributions, one of human capital and the other of wealth. Galbraith's research focuses on the impact of macroeconomic variables on inequality, both in the short and long runs. Also, during the period between 1970 and 1996 a number of econometric model builders working in international institutions and in some European universities developed groundbreaking research on bridging the gap with an assortment of short- and long-term econometric models. The models developed are very detailed, and much too advanced for this book, and so in an effort to capture the essence of the kind of thinking that has been used for some of the more detailed models, in this chapter we introduce two simple models: one based on integrating income distribution with long-term models of potential GDP and the other based on integrating income distribution with shorter-term input-output models.

13.1 Long-term Models

When most economists project the long term, their models generally project between 3 to 15 years. The long term for demographers is much longer, sometimes 50 years or more. As we know from chapter 10, empirical estimates of the Kuznets curve indicate that quintile shares of income change very slowly over long periods, much like the periods that demographers consider the long term.

Hence, in order to integrate long-term macroeconomic models with income distribution models, it is necessary to extend projections of the major economic variables over much longer periods than economists would ordinarily attempt. The linking variable between the two sets of data will be per capita GDP, which is used as a proxy for the level of development. While there is much controversy over the relationship between income shares and per capita GDP in the short run, that is, periods of fifteen years or shorter, the long-term empirical evidence based on cross-country analysis indicates a reasonably good relationship.

It is difficult to test the long-term relationship using a time series of income distribution data because no country but the United States has a longtime series of income distribution data. Even that series suffers from inconsistencies due to periodic changes in sampling practices. However, the U.S. data do indicate a rather strong linear relationship between the share of GDP flowing to the bottom 60% of the population (and top 20% as well) and the level of GDP. Unfortunately, the slope coefficient is negative, suggesting that the share flowing to the bottom 60% *decreases* as per capita income increases. This can be seen in table 13.1.

The equation predicts that when the per capita GDP reaches $42,674 (constant 1975 dollars), which would be sometime in the year 2059 if the long-term trend in the growth of per capita GDP persists on growing at an annual rate of 2% (third equation in table 13.1), the share of income flowing to the bottom 60% of households will dwindle to 0! Does this mean that sometime in the future that share will be 0? We do not think that anyone believes that; at one point, it will have to bottom out and perhaps reverse itself.

However, the equations estimated in table 13.1 also indicate that when the per capita income in the United States reaches about $15,888 (constant 1975 dollars), which should occur sometime in 2,010, the income shares of the bottom 60% and the top 5% will be equal. This does not seem so far-fetched since the difference in 2001 was only 4.4%. But what is curious about the U.S. case is that the curve seems to be on the wrong side of the Kuznets inverted U-curve.

At the level of economic development of the United States, one would think that the slope should be positive. This might be explained if one thinks of the development process capable of restarting itself when radical new technology is introduced. In such a case, relatively few members of the labor force could benefit from the higher wages in the new modern sector. Other people who would benefit from the new technology would be the investors and venture capitalists who finance it. This latter group are often members of the top 5.

If at the same time there is a significant immigration of people with traditional skills from lesser-developed countries, then chances are that they will not be employable in the new modern sector and probably end up in the

Table 13.1 U.S. Share of Total Income Flowing to the Richest 5% (T5) and the Bottom 60% (B60) of Households and Constant GDP per Capita (Y/P) in 1975 Dollars

Year	B60	T5	Y/P	Year	B60	T5	Y/P
2001	26.8	22.4	13,279	1983	30.6	16.4	8,789
2000	27.3	22.1	13,378	1982	30.8	16.2	8,501
1999	27.4	21.5	13,006	1981	31.2	15.6	8,760
1998	27.6	21.4	12,605	1980	31.5	15.8	8,661
1997	27.5	21.7	12,199	1979	31.4	16.4	8,738
1996	27.8	21.4	11,794	1978	31.5	16.2	8,563
1995	28.0	21.0	11,492	1977	31.7	16.1	8,202
1994	27.5	21.2	11,300	1976	31.9	16.0	7,917
1993	27.7	21.0	10,969	1975	32.0	15.9	7,589
1992	29.0	18.6	10,800	1974	32.1	15.9	7,674
1991	29.3	18.1	10,600	1973	31.8	16.6	7,790
1990	29.4	18.6	10,765	1972	31.7	17.0	7,436
1989	29.1	18.9	10,692	1971	32.0	16.7	7,129
1988	29.4	18.3	10,428	1970	32.3	16.6	7,081
1987	29.5	18.2	10,101	1969	32.5	16.6	7,055
1986	29.8	17.5	9,857	1968	32.8	16.6	6,914
1985	30.0	17.0	9,620	1967	32.1	17.5	6,665
1984	30.4	16.5	9,346				

Regression Results:
$B60 = 38.83342 - 0.00091 Y/P$, adjusted $R^2 = .951$
$\quad (t = 111.8) \quad (t = -25.7)$
$T5 = 8.550298 + 0.000996 Y/P$, adjusted $R^2 = .792$
$\quad (t = 10.0) \quad (t = 11.4)$
$\ln(Y/P) = -30.7136 + .020091$ year, $R^2 = .988$
$\quad (t = -41.4) \quad (t = 53.7)$

Note: Shares of total income are based on quintile shares in appendix II.

bottom 60. Since their incomes will be tied to the minimum wage, the shares of the top 5 and bottom 60 could switch from trending toward more equality to more inequality. There is some evidence that the United States was on the right-hand side of the U-curve from 1967 to 1981. During that period the share of the top 5 decreased from 17.5% down to 15.6% (see table 13.1). However, the share of the bottom 60 also declined slightly during that period, from 32.1% to 31.2%. This means that the top 5 were giving up share to the 35% of households above the bottom 60 but below the top 5. You might think of this group as the upper middle class.

In 1981 this trend stopped. The bottom 60 continued to lose share, but the top 5 started gaining share again. As far as the upper middle class goes, they started in 1967 with a share of 50.4%, went up to a share of 53.1% in 1984, and then began a slide to 50.8% in 2001. Two contributing factors in the United States to these trends might be the unusually high incomes of CEOs of some of the larger corporations in the United States and change in technology brought about by the widespread use of personal computers, which began around 1984.

In an article of the April 28, 2003, issue of *Fortune*[1] it is pointed out that during the 2000 to 2002 period, chairman and CEO salaries and bonuses increased by 32%, whereas the salaries of top marketing executives decreased by 13%. Even as companies' stocks declined, most CEOs continued to enjoy increases in pay. The article also makes the point that

> [t]he situation wasn't always so. Up through the 1970s, a chief executive's pay was generally linked to that of his underlings in a geometrically proportional relationship known as the "golden triangle." But soon a new breed of compensation consultant began whispering in CEOs' ears: Look what the other chiefs are making. They pointed to a "peer group" and calculated the average pay. Because some of those peers were likely to have supersized salaries, just pegging the CEO's pay to the average usually guaranteed a raise.

This probably explains a good portion of the differences between the income shares of the top 5 and the upper middle class from 1967 to 2001.

Long-term Assumptions on GDP and Population

Over long periods of time, we will assume that gross domestic product will lie on its potential growth path. In any particular year the economy can depart from potential, but this will be temporary, and a return to potential will eventually follow. When the economy is above potential, the labor market will tighten, pushing the unemployment rate below the natural rate of employment. We will assume the reverse when GDP is below potential. To arrive at GDP per person, which will be the proxy for level of development, we will assume that there is some correlation between the level of development and the growth of population, but the lags are long, and it is probably better to let population projections be done by demographers and treat it as exogenous.

One source of population projections is the Population Division of the United Nations Department of Economic and Social Affairs. Thus, we arrive at per capita GDP by dividing the projection for GDP by the projection for population. One way to project potential GDP would be to estimate the exponential growth trend model by taking logarithms of both sides of the equation and using linear regression to estimate the parameters. For example, the exponential growth rate model is given by:

$$GDP = ae^{bt},$$

where GDP is expressed in constant prices of some base year and t indexes time (years for the long term). The a parameter in the above equation is the value of GDP at time 0. The b parameter is the instantaneous compound growth rate of GDP.

---

[1]*Have They No Shame?*, Fortune, April 28, 2003, p. 58.

Table 13.2 U.S. Gross Domestic Product in Constant 1975
Dollars (Billions)

Year	GDP	Year	GDP	Year	GDP	Year	GDP
1967	1,324.5	1976	1,726.2	1985	2,289.9	1994	2,941.7
1968	1,387.7	1977	1,806.3	1986	2,367.0	1995	3,020.2
1969	1,429.8	1978	1,905.9	1987	2,447.5	1996	3,128.0
1970	1,432.5	1979	1,966.6	1988	2,549.6	1997	3,266.7
1971	1,480.4	1980	1,962.1	1989	2,639.0	1998	3,406.6
1972	1,560.7	1981	2,010.2	1990	2,685.5	1999	3,546.7
1973	1,650.8	1982	1,969.5	1991	2,672.9	2000	3,679.8
1974	1,641.0	1983	2,054.7	1992	2,754.4	2001	3,689.0
1975	1,635.2	1984	2,204.0	1993	2,827.5	2002	3,779.3

Regression Results:
$\ln(\text{GDP}) = -51.69494 + 0.029938t$, adjusted $R^2 = .9954$
$\qquad\qquad (-75.32)\quad (86.57)$

Taking natural logarithms of both sides yields:

$$\ln(\text{GDP}) = a + bt.$$

The regression result in table 13.2 is the 1967 to 2002 GDP trend equation for the United States based on 1975 constant dollars. To get a projection to the year 2025, we replace t in the equation by 2025, which yields: $\ln(\text{GDP}) = -51.69494 + 0.029938(2025) = 8.92951$. The exponential (anti-log) of 8.92951 is $7,551.5642 billion.

The UN projection[2] of the U.S. population for 2025 comes in three scenarios: low, 303.132 million; medium, 332.481 million; and high, 354.649 million. Under the low scenario the estimated GDP per capita would be $24,912; under the medium scenario, $22,713; and under the high scenario, $21,293.

Long-term Assumptions on Income Shares

The smooth curve in figure 13.1 is a plot of potential GDP based on the trend equation shown in table 13.2. The fluctuating curve winding around potential GDP is the actual GDP (in billions of 1975 dollars). If we use the share equations in table 13.1 to project the shares of the total income flowing to the bottom 60% and top 5% of the households, we get:

1. Low population scenario: B60 = 38.83342 − 0.00091(24912) = 16.2%
                                   T5 = 8.550298 + .000996(24912) = 33.4%
2. Medium population scenario: B60 = 38.83342 − 0.00091(22713) = 18.2%
                                   T5 = 8.550298 + .000996(22713) = 31.2%
3. High population scenario: B60 = 38.83342 − 0.00091(21293) = 19.5%
                                   T5 = 8.550298 + .000996(21293) = 29.8%

[2]United Nations, *World Population Prospects*, 1996 revision, 1998.

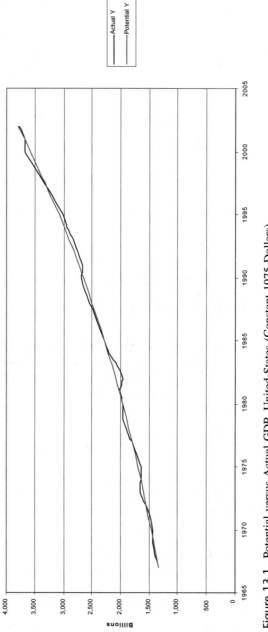

Figure 13.1. Potential versus Actual GDP, United States (Constant 1975 Dollars)

The income share projections to the year 2025 indicate some interesting but not very believable results. All three scenarios on population growth rate lead to much lower shares of income flowing to the bottom 60% of households than to the top 5%. The differences are so large that it does not seem possible that the U.S. population would tolerate such a deterioration in income equality. While the regression equations for the shares (see table 13.1) fit very tightly, the trend will most likely reverse itself between 2003 and 2025.

An alternative projection would be to use the equation for the bottom 60% based upon the Kuznets hypothesis from chapter 10. Since data are available for 2001, we can pass that year into the equation to set the constant coefficient for the United States. Hence we get:

$$B60 = X - 17.07(\ln Y/P) + 1.36(\ln Y/P)^2.$$

From table 13.1 :

$$26.8 = X - 17.07(\ln 13,279) + 1.36(\ln 13,279)^2$$
$$26.8 = X - 162.06154 + 122.58344$$
$$X = 66.278104.$$

For the medium scenario we get:

$$B60 \text{ in } 2025 = 66.278104 - 17.07(\ln 22,713) + 1.36(\ln 22,713)^2$$
$$B60 \text{ in } 2025 = 66.278104 - 171.22392 + 136.83612 = 31.89\%.$$

This last estimate is more in line with the share of total income that the bottom 60% had in the early 1970s and seems more plausible.

13.2 Short-term Models

From the point of view of income distribution, we will regard periods of less than fifteen years as the short term. In the short term there are a number of variables that might cause income distribution to fluctuate around its long-term trend. Income distribution may be affected by government tax and social welfare policies, growth or lack of growth in sectors of the economy that only certain income groups of households draw their livelihood, general economic recession, and general economic expansion. In the case of general economic recession, the bottom 60% of the households may improve or worsen their share of the total household income, depending on what kind of stabilizers are working for their income protection.

For example, if there is comprehensive unemployment insurance, which provides income to households of displaced workers caught in a downturn of the economy, it could actually improve their share of income as long as the top 5% does not qualify for unemployment benefits. However, while the share of income for the bottom 60% may increase, they may actually suffer a decline in real income because the unemployment benefits received may not be as much as their normal income. Government spending on social variables such as education and health tends to improve income distribution, and government spending on military tends to worsen income distribution.

Military spending may lead to excessive government investment on military hardware such as tanks and airplanes, which does not contribute to as much growth to the economy as the same amount of investment in the civilian economy usually does. Furthermore, excessive government spending on military investment may crowd out investment in the private sector because it could drive up interest rates. In the short term, a number of economic and social variables can interact with one another in complicated ways to yield different results on income distribution. Hence, it is necessary to use much more detailed models to capture these effects.

Prominent among these models are the social accounting models (SAMs), which incorporate social and economic variables into a simulation that is designed to test different socioeconomic policy mixes. Much work on SAMs and related models has been done by international institutions such as the World Bank (see Pyatt [9]) and the International Labor Office (see Hopkins and Van der Hoven [7]), and in universities (for example, see Lenti [8]). Erasmus University in the Netherlands has been one of the leading research centers on SAMs, where Suleiman I. Cohen [4] and others there have built SAM models for many developing countries including Korea and Pakistan. Perhaps the best approach to understanding SAM modeling is to first understand how input-output models function.

Input-Output Models of the Economy

Input-output models were developed by Wassily Leontief[3] to show the interdependence of industry in an economy. An input-output model shows the use of output of each industry as inputs by other industries and for final consumption. It assumes that at least for the short run any industry's inputs are a fixed proportion of its output. Hence, if output for a particular industry is increased, then all its inputs from other industries (including its own industry) will increase in fixed proportions.

For example, it shows how the increase in demand for trucks will lead to an increase in the demand for steel, glass, tires, plastic, upholstery materials, and so on, and how the increase for these products will lead to an increase in the demand for the inputs needed to produce them. To show these relationships, Leontief developed the input-output table, which is a rectangular matrix whose rows are the supplying industries and whose columns are the producing industries.

Table 13.3 gives the input-output table for a fictitious economy divided into three major producing sectors—agriculture, industry, and services. It shows

---

[3]Leontief received the Nobel Prize in Economics in 1973.

Table 13.3 Three Industry Input-Output Flow Table
(Billions of Dollars)

Supplying Industry	Producing Industry			Final Demand	Sum
	Agriculture	Industry	Services		
Agriculture	20	60	30	90	200
Industry	80	90	20	110	300
Services	40	30	110	420	600
Value Added	60	120	440		
Total	200	300	600	620	

the flow of inputs and outputs among the industries. It also shows the final demand for the output of each industry as well as the value added by industry. For example, the first row shows that of a total output valued at $200 billion for agriculture, $110 billion represents sales of intermediate goods to other industries ($20 billion back into agriculture, $60 billion into industry, and $30 billion into services), and $90 billion goes to consumers for final consumption.

From the flow table 13.3 we will next derive the input-output coefficient table showing the fixed proportion each input is of the industry's output. Once again, we stress the assumption that these proportions remain valid only in the short term. These are shown in table 13.4. The columns of table 13.4 can be interpreted as linear production functions in which the factor inputs are complementary rather than substitutes. By dividing the input requirements shown in each column of table 13.3 by the column total, we get the *direct requirements matrix* of coefficients shown in table 13.4. For example, the cefficients 0.1, 0.4, and 0.2 in the column under agriculture are obtained by dividing the values 20, 80, and 40 in table 13.3 by 200.

The coefficients in each column can also be interpreted as the input requirements needed to produce each dollar of output for the industry—thus, for each dollar of output in agriculture, 10 cents of input from agriculture (i.e., for seed), 40 cents of input from industry (i.e., for farm machinery), and 20 cents of input from services (i.e., for veterinarians, insurance, accountants, etc.). Hence, for agriculture to increase its output by $100 million, it would need an additional $10 million of inputs from agriculture, $40 million of inputs from industry, and $20 million of inputs from services.

Table 13.4 Three Industry Input-Output Coefficient Table

Supplying Industry	Producing Industry		
	Agriculture	Industry	Services
Agriculture	0.1	0.2	0.05
Industry	0.4	0.3	0.0333
Services	0.2	0.1	0.1833

Under the assumption that the coefficients will not change, it is possible to estimate the levels of output that each industry must produce when the levels of final demand are specified. Since household consumption is a large part of final demand, the model makes it possible to test scenarios on the feasibility of channeling more consumption to households. While this will not answer the important question of how that consumption is distributed to those households, it does answer the question of what consumption is feasible for the average household.

To see how the model works, let FDA be the amount of desired final demand in agriculture, and FDI and FDS be the corresponding amounts for industry and services. The total outputs of the sectors agriculture, industry, and services are the unknowns that we will label as YA, YI, and YS, respectively. Then it follows:

$$0.1YA + 0.2YI + 0.0500YS + FDA = YA$$
$$0.4YA + 0.3YI + 0.0333YS + FDI = YI$$
$$0.2YA + 0.1YI + 0.1833YS + FDS = YS$$

Suppose, for example, that it was desired to increase FDA by $10 billion, FDI by $40 billion and FDS by $30 billion. Then FDA would equal $100 billion, FDI would equal $150 billion, and FDS would equal $450 billion. Substituting these numbers into the above equations, we get:

$$0.1YA + 0.2YI + 0.0500YS + 100 = YA$$
$$0.4YA + 0.3YI + 0.0333YS + 150 = YI$$
$$0.2YA + 0.1YI + 0.1833YS + 450 = YS$$

These equations can be put in the standard form for three equations with three unknowns and solved using elementary methods.

$$0.9YA - 0.2YI - 0.0500YS = 100$$
$$-.4YA + 0.7YI - 0.0333YS = 150$$
$$-.2YA + -.1YI + 0.8166YS = 450$$

The solution rounded off to the nearest billion dollars is:

$$YA = \$231 \text{ billion}$$
$$YI = \$378 \text{ billion}$$
$$YS = \$654 \text{ billion}$$

Social Accounting Matrices

Table 13.5 is an extension of the input-output flow table 13.3 to a SAM. Rows 4, 5 6, and 7 of table 13.5 show a more detailed breakdown of the value added in table 13.3.

Table 13.5 Social Accounting Matrix

| | Output Industries | | | | | | | | | | | Final | |
	1. Agri.	2. Ind.	3. Serv.	4. ECU	5. ECR	6. TAX	7. OVA	8. U-HH	9. R-HH	10. G	11. Oth.	Demand	Total
Supplying Industries													
1. Agriculture	20	60	30									90	200
2. Industry	80	90	20									110	300
3. Services	40	30	110									420	600
Value Added													
4. EC Urban HH	4	50	216										270
5. EC Rural HH	32	22	92										146
6. Taxes	6	18	30										54
7. Oth. Value Added	18	30	102										150
Gross Receipts													
8. Urban Households				270			20						290
9. Rural Households					146		10						156
10. Government						54		81	44		3		182
11. Others							120						120
Net Income													
12. Urban Households								174		35	43		252
13. Rural Households									90	23	25		138
14. Government										115			115
15. Other's Income								35	22	9	49		115
Total	200	300	600	270	146	54	150	290	156	182	120	620	

In rows 4 and 5, employee compensation from the three major producing sectors to urban and rural households was taken out of total value added in order to capture the income distribution between the two groups of households. Also, in order to show the government revenue coming from firms, taxes paid were also taken out of value added in row 6. Hence some of the $620 billion of value added is now shown in terms of its returns to factors, namely, employee compensation to urban and households. The rest goes to government taxes and a residual group in row 7 called *others*. However, rows 8 to 11 are needed to show the rest of the income received by households. This includes all transfers from other value added. Row 10 shows all the sources of Government revenue, including taxes from households. Finally, in rows 12 to 15, we see the after-tax transfers from government and others.

Before taxes the urban households have an income of $290 billion, and the rural households have an income of $156 billion. Hence the urban households have about 65% of the total household income. After taxes, the urban households have an income of $252 billion, and the rural households $138 billion. The share of the urban households decreases slightly to 64% of the total net household income.

Changing the Levels of Final Demand

Table 13.6 shows the resulting changes on the entire SAM when the changes in final demand in the input-output part of the SAM are implemented. If the levels of final demand are changed to FDA = $100 billion, FDI = $150 billion, and FDS = $450 billion, as was the case in the previous section on input-output models, we can then use our previous results, namely, YA = $231 billion, YI = $378 billion, and YS = $654 billion.

Furthermore, we can finish updating rows 1, 2, and 3 of the SAM by applying the input-output coefficients of table 13.4 to these totals. Now if we make the assumption that the employee compensation to urban and rural households will be in the same proportion to the new totals of YA, YI, and YS as they were in table 13.5, we will get rows 4 and 5 of table 13.6. Likewise, if we make the same assumption regarding taxes and other value added, we get rows 6 and 7 of table 13.6. Maintaining the same principle of fixed proportions for the remaining rows 8 to 15, we fill in the rest of the cells in the adjusted SAM found in table 13.6.

For example, row 8, which shows the total gross income of households, gets total employee compensation from the total on line 4 and the amount of income from other value added by taking the proportion of that figure to total value added in table 13.4 times the total of value added (row 7) in table 13.6. That is: (20/150)170 = 22.64. *Note*: this computation leads to 22.67, but 170 has been rounded up from 169.8. These computations were done in a spreadsheet, but not all the decimal places for the totals are shown. Similar

Table 13.6 Social Accounting Matrix

	Output Sectors											Final	
	1. Agri.	2. Ind.	3. Serv.	4. ECU	5. ECR	6. TAX	7. OVA	8. U-HH	9. R-HH	10. G	11. Oth.	Demand	Total
Supplying Industries													
1. Agriculture	23.1	75.6	32.7									100	231
2. Industry	92.4	113.4	21.78									150	378
3. Services	46.2	37.8	119.88									450	654
Value Added													
4. EC Urban HH	4.62	63	235.46										303
5. EC Rural HH	36.96	27.72	100.29										165
6. Taxes	6.93	22.68	32.7										62.3
7. Oth. Value Added	20.79	37.8	111.19										170
Gross Receipts													
8. Urban Households				303			22.64						326
9. Rural Households					165		11.32						176
10. Government						62.3		90.98	49.72		3.8		207
11. Others							135.8						136
Net Income													
12. Urban Households								195.43		39.77	48.51		284
13. Rural Households									101.71	26.14	28.2		156
14. Government										130.7			131
15. Other's Income								39.31	24.86	10.22	55.28		130
Total	231	378	654	303	165	62.3	169.8	325.72	176.29	206.8	135.8	700	

computations are made for the rest of the cells in the table. From table 13.6 we see that the levels of the gross and net incomes have risen, but the difference in the ratio of urban to rural income has only slightly changed.

Problems

1. Using the data in table 13.2, reestimate the long-term trend equation for GDP over the period 1980 to 2002. How does this growth rate compare with the growth rate of the longer period from 1967 to 2002?
2. From the equation estimated in problem 1, estimate the per capita income of the United States under the low, medium, and high scenario of population.
3. For each estimate of per capita GDP made in problem 2, estimate the share of income flowing to the bottom 60% and the top 5% of households using the equations:

$$B60 = 38.83342 - 0.00091 Y/P$$
$$T5 = 8.550298 + 0.000996 Y/P$$

4. Estimate the share of income flowing to the bottom 60% of households for each scenario of per capita income made in problem 2 for the following equation:

$$B60 = 66.278104 - 17.07 \ln(Y/P) + 1.36 \left[\ln(Y/P)\right]^2.$$

Use the coefficients in table 13.4 to estimate the levels of output in agriculture, industry, and services if it is desired to have a final demand of 90 for agriculture, 400 for industry, and 420 for services.

5. Adjust table 13.5 for the final demand and total outputs of problem 5. What is the ratio of incomes between urban and rural households?

References

1. Adelman, Irma and Sherman Robinson, *Income Distribution Policies in Developing Countries: A Case Study of Korea*, Stanford, Stanford University Press, 1978.
2. Adelman, I., M. Hopkins, G. Rodgers, R. Véry, *A Comparison of Two Models for Income Distribution Planning*, Journal of Policy Modelling, Vol. 1, 1979, pp. 37–82.
3. Civardi, Maisa B., *Income Multipliers in the Household Institutional Sector*, in C. Dagum and M. Zenga, eds., *Studies in Contemporary Economics: Income and Wealth Distribution, Inequality and Poverty*, Berlin, Springer-Verlag, 1990.
4. Cohen, Suleiman I., *Two Attempts to Extend Economic Models to Sociopolitical Issues and Realities*, Pakistan Development Review, Vol. 19, No. 4, Winter 1980, pp. 282–310.
5. Dagum, C., *Linking the Functional and Personal Distributions of Income*, in Jacque Silber, ed., *Handbook of Income Inequality Measurement*, Kluwer Academic Press, 1999.

6. Galbraith, James K., *Macroeconomics of Income Distributions*, in James K. Galbraith and Maureen Berner, eds., *Inequality and Change—A Global View*, Cambridge, Cambridge University Press, 2001.
7. Hopkins, M. and R.Van der Hoven, *Economic and Social Factors in Development: A Socio-economic Framework for Basic Needs Planning*, WEP 2-32/WP 32, Geneva, ILO, November 1981.
8. Lenti, Renata Targetti, *Income Distribution and the Structure of the Economic System: a SAM Approach*, in C. Dagum and M. Zenga, eds., *Studies in Contemporary Economics: Income and Wealth Distribution, Inequality and Poverty*, Berlin, Springer-Verlag, 1990.
9. Pyatt, G., *A SAM Approach to Modelling*, Journal of Policy Modelling, No. 3, 1988, pp. 327–352.
10. United Nations, *Handbook of Input-Output Table Compilation and Analysis*, New York, United Nations, 1999.

Appendix I

Quintile Shares and Upper Decile Share of Income—Per Capita Income
Given in 1990 U.S. Dollars

	Q1	Q2	Q3	Q4	Q5	D10	Y/P	Survey
ALGERIA	2.3	6.6	12.1	21	57.9	40.5	1,555.3	1968
ALGERIA	6.9	11	14.9	20.7	46.5	31.7	2,306.3	1988
ARGENTINA	5.1	9.3	13.1	18.6	53.9	40.7	4,581.8	1961
ARGENTINA	4.4	9.7	14.1	21.5	50.3	35.2	5,506.6	1970
AUSTRALIA	7.1	12.9	17.6	23.5	38.9	23.5	11,965.2	1968
AUSTRALIA	3.8	12.2	18.3	26	39.7	30.9	13,956.2	1976
AUSTRALIA	6.4	12.7	18.1	24.2	38.7	29.4	14,764.2	1979
AUSTRALIA	4.4	11.1	17.5	24.8	42.2	25.8	16,454.6	1985
AUSTRIA	5.1	10.3	15.4	22.5	46.7	30.5	14,614.5	1974
AUSTRIA	4.7	9.5	16.5	24.1	45.1	28.7	15,031.7	1976
BAHRAIN	4.6	8.8	13.2	19.9	53.5	38.2	9,439.1	1984
BANGLADESH	7.9	11.7	15.8	22.3	42.3	26.7	160.2	1967
BANGLADESH	6.6	11	15.1	21.1	46.3	31.2	148.4	1974
BANGLADESH	6.2	10.9	15	21	46.9	32	143	1977
BANGLADESH	6.2	10.5	14.6	20.8	48.1	33	165.3	1982
BANGLADESH	9.5	13.4	17	21.6	38.6	24.6	187.5	1988
BARBADOS	4	10.7	15.8	22.6	46.9	31.1	3,917.7	1970
BELGIUM	4.5	10.5	15.8	22.4	46.8	31.1	13,916.6	1975
BELGIUM	7.9	13.7	18.6	23.8	36	21.5	15,103.9	1978
BENIN	5.5	10.3	13.9	18.6	51.7	39.3	15,103.9	1959
BOLIVIA	5.6	9.7	14.5	22	48.2	31.7	841.2	1990
BOTSWANA	4	7.5	11	17.1	60.4	46.5	1,262.1	1975
BOTSWANA	4.3	7.7	12	18.4	57.6	42	1,703.3	1982
BOTSWANA	3.6	6.9	11.4	19.2	58.9	42.9	2,072.4	1985
BRAZIL	2	5	9.4	17	66.6	50.6	2,218.2	1972
BRAZIL	2.3	5.9	10.3	17.9	63.7	48.3	3,014.3	1982
BRAZIL	2.1	4.9	8.9	16.8	67.5	51.3	3,293.3	1989
BULGARIA	9.7	14.7	17.9	21.8	36	22.5	4,484.9	1982
BULGARIA	10.4	13.9	17.3	22.2	36.2	21.9	4,617.3	1992
BURMA	5.8	10.1	14	19.5	50.6	30.1	512.8	1970

(continued)

Quintile Shares and Upper Decile Share of Income—Per Capita Income
Given in 1990 U.S. Dollars (*continued*)

	Q1	Q2	Q3	Q4	Q5	D10	Y/P	Survey
CANADA	3.8	10.7	17.9	25.6	42	23.4	16,384.6	1977
CANADA	4.6	11	17.7	25.2	41.6	25	17,880.1	1981
CANADA	5.7	11.8	17.7	24.6	40.2	24.1	19,894.5	1987
CHILE	4.4	9	13.8	21.4	51.3	34.8	1,646.7	1968
CHILE	3.7	6.8	10.3	16.2	62.9	48.9	2,265.5	1989
CHINA	6.4	11	16.4	24.4	41.8	24.6	319.8	1990
COLOMBIA	2.8	7	12.1	18.6	59.4	44.6	794.3	1970
COLOMBIA	3.6	7.6	12.6	20.4	55.8	39.5	1,251.2	1991
COSTA RICA	4.8	9.5	13.6	21.7	50.4	33.8	1,641.1	1971
COSTA RICA	4	9.1	14.3	21.9	50.8	34.1	1,863.9	1989
COTE D'IVOIRE	3.9	6.7	11.2	19.7	58.5	41.5	1,714.8	1970
COTE D'IVOIRE	7.3	11.9	16.3	22.3	42.2	26.9	1,577.6	1988
CYPRUS	11.3	15.9	19.3	23.1	30.4	16.9	2,664.7	1966
CYPRUS	4.5	11.5	17.5	24.4	42.1	25.9	5,743.3	1984
CZECHOSLOVKIA	12	15.6	19	22.4	31	16.8	5,142.2	1970
CZECHOSLOVKIA	11.9	15.5	18.7	22.8	31.1	17.4	6,481.7	1975
CZECHOSLOVKIA	10	14.4	17.7	22.1	35.8	21.8	7,749.5	1981
DENMARK	5.4	12	18.4	25.6	38.6	22.3	20,630.6	1981
DOM.REPUBLIC	4.3	8.1	12.8	20.5	54.3	38	633	1969
DOM.REPUBLIC	4.5	8.2	12.1	18.6	56.5	41.7	1,016.6	1977
DOM.REPUBLIC	4.2	7.9	12.5	19.7	55.6	39.6	1,077.9	1989
EGYPT	4.6	9.5	14.6	22.9	48.4	31.1	497.3	1964
EGYPT	7.2	12.2	16.5	22.2	41.9	26.9	904	1990
EL SALVADOR	3.7	8.7	14	22.8	50.8	33	1,095.5	1969
EL SALVADOR	5.5	10	14.8	22.4	47.4	29.5	1,290	1977
ETHIOPIA	6.4	10.9	14.9	19.9	48	36.3	131	1970
ETHIOPIA	8.6	12.7	16.4	21.1	41.3	27.5	130.3	1981
FIJI	5.1	9.7	14.7	22.8	47.7	30.6	1,430.5	1972
FINLAND	2.7	10	17.3	26.4	43.6	21.2	18,273	1977
FINLAND	6.3	12.1	18.4	25.5	37.6	21.7	21,700	1981
FRANCE	4.3	9.8	16.3	22.7	46.9	30.4	13,461.7	1970
FRANCE	4.2	10	15.7	23	47.1	30.7	15,279.7	1975
FRANCE	5.6	11.8	17.2	23.5	41.9	26.1	20,637.3	1989
GABON	3.2	5.3	8.8	15.2	67.5	54.7	5,949	1968
GERMANY (FRG)	5.9	10.5	15.3	22.7	45.6	29.1	11,855.4	1970
GERMANY (FRG)	6	12	17.9	24.5	39.6	24	14,605.1	1978
GERMANY (FRG)	7	11.8	17.1	23.9	40.3	24.4	17,503.9	1988
GHANA	7.6	12.9	17.3	22.9	39.3	24.2	524.2	1969
GHANA	7	11.3	15.8	21.8	44.1	29	405.5	1988
GREECE	6.3	11.1	15.6	22.3	44.7	29	405.5	1958
GREECE	6.6	12.5	16.2	20.9	43.8	29.5	4,875.9	1974
GUATEMALA	3.6	7.7	11.6	19.1	58	35.8	729.8	1970
GUATEMALA	5.3	8.4	11.9	18	56.4	42.1	974.8	1981
GUATEMALA	2.1	5.8	10.5	18.6	63	46.6	827.1	1989
GUINEA-BISSAU	2.1	6.5	12	20.6	58.9	42.4	244.4	1991
GUYANA	4.3	10.3	15.7	23.2	46.5	29.8	244.4	1956
HONDURAS	1.3	3.8	7.2	13.8	73.9	60.6	1,060.9	1968
HONDURAS	2.7	6	10.2	17.6	63.5	47.9	1,243.3	1989
HONG KONG	5.6	10	14.3	21.1	49	33.7	4,131	1971

Quintile Shares and Upper Decile Share of Income—Per Capita Income
Given in 1990 U.S. Dollars (*continued*)

	Q1	Q2	Q3	Q4	Q5	D10	Y/P	Survey
HONG KONG	4.8	10.2	14.4	20.4	50.2	34.8	5,507	1976
HONG KONG	5.4	10.8	15.2	21.6	47	31.3	7,425.7	1980
HUNGARY	9.1	15	19	23.5	33.4	19.1	5,287.9	1975
HUNGARY	10.9	14.8	18	22	34.4	20.8	6,894	1989
INDIA	6.7	10.5	14.3	19.6	48.9	35.2	225.3	1964
INDIA	7	9.2	13.9	20.5	49.4	35.2	239.4	1975
INDIA	8.8	12.5	16.2	21.3	41.3	27.1	344.2	1989
INDONESIA	6.8	10.5	13.4	17.3	52	40.7	253.5	1971
INDONESIA	6.6	7.8	12.6	23.6	49.4	34	325.6	1976
INDONESIA	8.7	12.1	15.9	21.1	42.3	27.9	581	1990
IRAN	2.7	5.5	9.6	16.8	65.4	51.2	13,934.5	1975
IRAQ	2.1	4.4	8.8	17.8	66.9	49.8	13,934.5	1956
IRELAND	4.6	10.8	16.9	24.4	43.3	26.5	9,256.1	1980
ISRAEL	4.7	11.3	17	23.8	43.3	26.9	7,645.4	1969
ISRAEL	5.6	12.4	18	24.5	39.5	23.5	9,958.6	1976
ISRAEL	6	12.1	17.8	24.5	39.6	23.5	10,048.4	1979
ITALY	6.5	11.7	16.6	23	42.2	26.6	13,329.2	1976
ITALY	6.8	12	16.7	23.5	41	25.3	16,932.6	1986
JAMAICA	2.2	6	10.8	19.8	61.2	43.8	16,932.6	1958
JAMAICA	6	9.9	14.5	21.3	48.4	32.6	1,688	1990
JAPAN	8.2	12.7	17	22.8	39.3	24.2	13,389.1	1972
JAPAN	8.7	13.2	17.5	23.1	37.5	22.4	16,452.5	1979
JORDAN	9	14.4	18.3	23	35.3	21	958.7	1986
JORDAN	6.5	10.3	14.6	20.9	47.7	32.6	863.6	1991
KENYA	4.7	10.2	14	20.1	51	36.1	321.3	1977
KENYA	3.4	6.7	10.7	17.3	61.8	47.9	350.7	1992
KOREA	8.1	13.1	17.1	22.4	39.3	24.2	2,764.4	1981
KOREA	7.7	12.8	16.7	22.4	40.3	25.1	3,677	1985
KOREA	7.4	12.3	16.3	21.8	42.2	27.6	5,006.1	1988
LESOTHO	2.9	6.4	11.3	19.5	60	43.6	263.7	1986
LESOTHO	1	4.6	10.1	19.5	64.8	47.8	296.8	1988
LIBYA	10.1	13.5	17.1	22.4	36.9	22.2	12,343	1962
MADAGASCAR	5.2	7.8	11	15.9	60.1	48.6	337.8	1960
MALAWI	2.3	5	8	13.9	70.9	58.1	236.4	1980
MALAYSIA	3.5	7.7	12.5	20.3	56	39.9	893	1970
MALAYSIA	4.6	8.3	13	20.4	53.7	37.9	2,233.3	1989
MAURITANIA	3.5	10.7	16.2	23.3	46.3	30.2	533.9	1987
MAURITIUS	4	7.5	11	17	60.5	46.7	1,544.8	1981
MEXICO	3.5	7.9	13.2	21.6	53.8	39.1	2,673.2	1977
MEXICO	4.1	7.8	12.3	19.9	55.9	39.5	3,046.5	1984
MOROCCO	3.4	7.8	12.7	20	55.9	40.2	654.3	1971
MOROCCO	6.6	10.5	15	21.7	46.3	30.5	1,066.9	1990
NEPAL	6.5	10.8	14.9	20.9	47	31.9	148.5	1977
NEPAL	9.1	12.9	16.7	21.8	39.5	25	140.9	1984
NETHERLANDS	8.1	13.3	17.7	22.8	38.1	23.3	15,790.8	1977
NETHERLANDS	7.1	13.8	17.7	23.1	38.9	23.9	16,017.4	1981
NETHERLANDS	8.2	13.1	18.1	23.7	36.9	21.9	17,691.7	1988
NEW ZEALAND	5.7	12.1	17.2	23.7	41.3	25.4	11,103.6	1972
NEW ZEALAND	5.1	10.8	16.2	23.2	44.7	28.7	12,295.8	1981

(*continued*)

Quintile Shares and Upper Decile Share of Income—Per Capita Income
Given in 1990 U.S. Dollars (*continued*)

	Q1	Q2	Q3	Q4	Q5	D10	Y/P	Survey
NEW ZEALAND	5.3	11.5	17	23.6	42.6	26.7	13,180.1	1988
NIGER	4.7	9.6	14.6	21.8	49.4	33.3	274.5	1973
NIGERIA	5.4	9.2	13.3	19.2	52.9	38.7	341	1970
NORWAY	4.7	12.4	17.6	24.3	41	25	10,977.3	1963
NORWAY	4.3	11.3	18.1	25.2	41	24.3	17,440.4	1976
NORWAY	6.2	12.8	18.9	25.3	36.7	21.2	19,461	1979
NORWAY	5	12	17.9	25.1	40	23.7	20,491.5	1982
PAKISTAN	6.4	11.1	15.5	21.7	45.3	30.2	180.9	1964
PAKISTAN	8	12.5	16.1	22.1	41.4	27	234.5	1971
PAKISTAN	7.4	11.5	15.2	20.9	45	30.3	296	1979
PAKISTAN	8.4	12.9	16.9	22.2	39.7	25.2	403.9	1991
PANAMA	4.6	10.6	15.5	21.9	47.4	32.2	2,086.1	1972
PANAMA	2	6.3	11.6	20.3	59.8	42.1	2,074.6	1989
PERU	1.9	5.1	11	21	61	42.9	2,454.6	1972
PERU	4.9	9.2	13.7	21	51.4	35.4	2,221.9	1985
PHILIPPINES	5.5	9.2	12.9	19.1	53.3	38.8	648.8	1975
PHILIPPINES	6.5	10.1	14.4	21.2	47.8	32.1	694	1988
POLAND	9.8	13.6	17.5	23	36.1	21.2	5,946.4	1975
POLAND	10.1	14.5	18.1	22.6	34.7	20.6	4,552.7	1983
POLAND	9.2	13.8	17.9	23	36.1	21.6	5,268.9	1989
PORTUGAL	5.9	11.2	14.6	20.1	48.2	34.4	4,232.2	1974
REUNION	3.1	6.2	9.6	16	65.2	51.4	2,291.9	1977
RWANDA	9.7	13.1	16.7	21.6	38.9	24.6	384.7	1983
SENEGAL	3.2	6.2	10.4	17.7	62.5	47.8	785.1	1960
SENEGAL	3.5	7	11.6	19.3	58.6	42.8	879.3	1991
SEYCHELLES	4.1	9	14	21.3	51.6	35.6	3,654.1	1978
SINGAPORE	6.5	10.3	14	20	49.2	34.4	6,279.6	1978
SINGAPORE	5.1	9.9	14.6	21.4	48.9	33.5	8,409.3	1982
SIERRA LEONE	2	6.4	11.4	18.6	61.6	46.9	143.8	1969
SOUTH AFRICA	1.8	4.9	10.2	21.1	62	40.9	2,345.1	1965
SPAIN	6	10.5	15.4	22.6	45.5	29.3	5,981	1965
SPAIN	5.9	11.8	16.8	23.1	42.4	26.8	9,402.9	1974
SPAIN	6.9	12.5	17.3	23.4	40	24.6	9,541.4	1981
SPAIN	8.3	13.7	18.1	23.4	36.6	21.8	11,546.9	1988
SRI LANKA	7.3	12	16.1	21.8	42.8	30.6	274.6	1973
SRI LANKA	6.1	10.8	15	21.2	46.9	31.7	374.3	1981
SRI LANKA	8.9	13.1	16.9	21.7	39.3	25.2	460.7	1990
SUDAN	6.9	10.5	14.6	20	48.5	33.8	1,102	1968
SURINAM	9.3	12	15.5	21.2	42	27.3	1,881.5	1962
SWEDEN	5.2	11	16.2	23.5	44.1	27.5	19,390.7	1970
SWEDEN	8	13.2	17.4	24.5	36.9	20.8	22,529	1981
SWITZERLAND	5.2	11.7	16.4	22.1	44.6	29.8	28,496.2	1982
TAIWAN	8.8	13.5	17.5	23	37.2	22.4	2,453.1	1972
THAILAND	5.7	7.5	11.1	18.2	57.5	42.6	357.8	1962
THAILAND	5.1	8.2	11.7	17.9	57.1	42.8	704.7	1976
THAILAND	3.4	6.7	10.5	17.1	62.2	47.8	1,057.5	1986
THAILAND	6.1	9.4	13.5	20.3	50.7	35.3	1,263.3	1988
TRIN.&TOBAGO	4.2	9.1	13.9	22.8	50	33	4,287.5	1975
TUNISIA	4.2	8.1	12.3	19	56.3	41.2	1,121.9	1975

Quintile Shares and Upper Decile Share of Income—Per Capita Income
Given in 1990 U.S. Dollars (*continued*)

	Q1	Q2	Q3	Q4	Q5	D10	Y/P	Survey
TUNISIA	5.9	10.4	15.3	22.1	46.3	30.7	1,522.3	1990
TURKEY	3.5	7.9	12.5	19.4	56.7	41.5	1,298.6	1973
UGANDA	5	8.9	12.8	19	54.3	35.8	450.2	1970
UGANDA	8.5	12.1	16	21.5	41.9	27.2	204.9	1989
UNITD KINGDOM	6.6	11.9	17	24.2	40.3	23.9	10,859.7	1968
UNITD KINGDOM	5.8	11	17.6	24.7	41	24.8	13,391.3	1982
UNITD KINGDOM	4.6	10	16.8	24.3	44.3	27.8	16,718.7	1988
U.R. TANZANIA	5.8	10.2	13.9	19.7	50.4	35	103	1969
U.R. TANZANIA	5.3	9	13.1	19.2	53.4	39.4	114.4	1975
U.R. TANZANIA	2.4	5.7	10.4	18.7	62.7	46.5	100.1	1991
U.S.A.	4.4	10.5	17.1	24.8	43.3	26.9	16,560.2	1975
U.S.A.	4.3	10.3	16.9	24.8	43.7	27.4	18,513.5	1978
U.S.A.	4.0	9.7	16.3	24.6	45.3	29.1	20,155.8	1985
U.S.A.	3.9	9.6	15.9	24.0	46.6	30.4	21,827	1990
URUGUAY	4.4	9.8	15.2	23.1	47.5	30.4	1,923.7	1967
URUGUAY	6	10.9	15.5	22.3	45.3	29.3	2,343.1	1983
VENEZUELA	3.6	9.4	14.2	20.8	52	36.4	4,231.7	1971
VENEZUELA	4.8	9.5	14.4	21.9	49.5	33.2	2,350.4	1989
YUGOSLAVIA	6.6	11.8	16.7	23.5	41.4	25.3	6,031.7	1968
YUGOSLAVIA	6.2	12.2	17.5	24.1	40	24	10,976.1	1978
ZAIRE	5.5	9.3	13.4	19.2	52.6	39.4	132.5	1970
ZAMBIA	5.4	7.6	11.1	17.7	58.2	39.9	132.5	1959
ZAMBIA	5.6	9.6	14.2	21	49.7	34.2	461.9	1991
ZIMBABWE	3.2	4.9	8.3	14.4	69.2	56.9	536.1	1968
ZIMBABWE	4.5	7.4	10.6	15.5	61.7	49.3	804.7	1975
ZIMBABWE	4	6.3	10	17.4	62.3	46.9	680.9	1990

Appendix II

United States: Historical Shares of Income by Quintile of Household

Year	Q1	Q2	Q3	Q4	Q5	T5
2001	3.5	8.7	14.6	23	50.1	22.4
2000	3.6	8.9	14.8	23	49.8	22.1
1999	3.6	8.9	14.9	23.2	49.4	21.5
1998	3.6	9	15	23.2	49.2	21.4
1997	3.6	8.9	15	23.2	49.4	21.7
1996	3.7	9	15.1	23.3	49	21.4
1995	3.7	9.1	15.2	23.3	48.7	21
1994	3.6	8.9	15	23.4	49.1	21.2
1993	3.6	9	15.1	23.5	48.9	21
1992	3.8	9.4	15.8	24.2	46.9	18.6
1991	3.8	9.6	15.9	24.2	46.5	18.1
1990	3.9	9.6	15.9	24	46.6	18.6
1989	3.8	9.5	15.8	24	46.8	18.9
1988	3.8	9.6	16	24.3	46.3	18.3
1987	3.8	9.6	16.1	24.3	46.2	18.2
1986	3.9	9.7	16.2	24.5	45.7	17.5
1985	4	9.7	16.3	24.6	45.3	17
1984	4.1	9.9	16.4	24.7	44.9	16.5
1983	4.1	10	16.5	24.7	44.7	16.4
1982	4.1	10.1	16.6	24.7	44.5	16.2
1981	4.2	10.2	16.8	25	43.8	15.6
1980	4.3	10.3	16.9	24.9	43.7	15.8
1979	4.2	10.3	16.9	24.7	44	16.4
1978	4.3	10.3	16.9	24.8	43.7	16.2
1977	4.4	10.3	17	24.8	43.6	16.1
1976	4.4	10.4	17.1	24.8	43.3	16
1975	4.4	10.5	17.1	24.8	43.2	15.9
1974	4.4	10.6	17.1	24.7	43.1	15.9
1973	4.2	10.5	17.1	24.6	43.6	16.6
1972	4.1	10.5	17.1	24.5	43.9	17

United States: Historical Shares of Income by Quintile of Household
(*continued*)

Year	Q1	Q2	Q3	Q4	Q5	T5
1971	4.1	10.6	17.3	24.5	43.5	16.7
1970	4.1	10.8	17.4	24.5	43.3	16.6
1969	4.1	10.9	17.5	24.5	43	16.6
1968	4.2	11.1	17.5	24.4	42.8	16.6
1967	4	10.8	17.3	24.2	43.8	17.5

Source: U.S. Census Bureau, *Money Income in the United States: 2001* (PGO–218), Washington, GPO, September 2002, table A–Z, p. 19.

Appendix III

Software Instructions

General

The accompanying compact disc (CD ROM) contains programs that are useful in fitting the income distributions presented in the text. It is necessary to copy the contents of the CD ROM into a directory on the hard drive in order for the programs to execute. This can be accomplished by:

Step 1. Click on the **START** button and select **Programs**. If the **MS-DOS** or the **COMMAND PROMPT** is listed among the programs, click on that. If neither one of these appears among the list of programs, click on **Accessories**. The **COMMAND PROMPT** should appear there.

Step 2. After the **COMMAND PROMPT** is clicked, a black window will appear with a flickering cursor next to the command prompt. Type **CD** and press the **ENTER** key on the keyboard. The command prompt will become **C:\>**. Now type **MD\YDIST** and press **ENTER**. This creates a directory named **YDIST** on the hard drive where the programs on the **CD ROM** will be copied. The name **YDIST** is arbitrary, you may name this directory anything you wish, as long as another directory of that name is not already on the hard drive.

Step 3. Type **CD\YDIST** and press **ENTER**. You will now be in the newly created directory. Next type **COPY D: *.*** if your **CD ROM** is on the **D drive**. If it is on another drive, use the letter of that drive. All the software on the **CD ROM** will be copied into the new directory.

Name	Description
Lognorm	Fits the Log-Normal Distribution
Log_log	Fits the Log-logistic Distribution
Sing_mad	Fits the Singh-Maddala Distribution
Dagum	Fits the Dagum Distribution
Champ	Fits the 5 parameter Champernowne Distribution
CDF_dag	Finds the number of income units below an income level using the Dagum model
CDF_cham	Finds the number of income units below an income level using the 5 parameter Champernowne model
P_gini	Computes an age-Gini coefficient using a quadratic fit. The quadratic fit must be done by regression before this program is run.
Theil	Computes a Theil entropy inequality measure using a Dagum Distribution

To run a program in the directory it is only necessary to go into the directory, as in step 3 above, and type the name of the program and press **ENTER**.

For questions about this software, please contact Fred Campano at campano@fordham.edu.

Printing Results

The fitting programs will create a temporary file named **FORT15**, which is stored in the **YDIST** directory. The file is a text file that contains the screen output of the program. To print the file, use either **WORDPAD** or **NOTEPAD**, both of which are found in **Accessories**. Use the **OPEN** option found under the **FILE** button to access **FORT15** by typing **C:\YDIST\FORT15**. The output will appear and it will be possible to edit it before printing it out.

Inputting the Summary Tables

The fitting programs require that the summary table of the income distribution be typed into the program before they compute the parameters of the model. The example below illustrates this for all the fitting programs.

Consider the following table:

Male Full-time Year-Round Workers 1999

Income Class ($)	Interval Number
1–5,000	698
5,000–10,000	1,009
10,000–15,000	3,217
15,000–25,000	9,944
25,000–35,000	10,712
35,000–50,000	12,457
50,000–75,000	10,914
75,000+	8,569

Notice that there are eight income classes in the table.

Each fitting program will start off with the following message:

```
ENTER NUM. OF CLASSES IF EQ 0 STOP _
```

In the case of this distribution, type "8" and then press Enter. The screen will then appear like this:

```
ENTER NUM. OF CLASSES IF EQ 0 STOP 8
ENTER NAME OF COUNTRY AND YEAR OF SURVEY _
```

Type in the name of the distribution and press Enter (i.e. Male Full-time Year-Round Workers 1999). The screen will then appear like this:

```
ENTER NUM. OF CLASSES IF EQ 0 STOP 8
ENTER NAME OF COUNTRY AND YEAR OF SURVEY Male
Full-time Year-Round Workers 1999
ENTER CRITICAL VALUE OF CHI_SQUARE _
```

Next enter some low number such as "1." The screen will now appear like this:

```
ENTER NUM. OF CLASSES IF EQ 0 STOP 8
ENTER NAME OF COUNTRY AND YEAR OF SURVEY Male
Full-time Year-Round Workers 1999
ENTER CRITICAL VALUE OF CHI_SQUARE 1
ENTER INCOME CLASS ENDPOINTS FOR CLASSES 1 to 8
```

Enter the numbers at the beginning of each income class leaving a space between them, for example:

1 5000 10000 15000 25000 35000 50000 75000

(Note: In this case there should be eight numbers. Don't forget to press Enter after the last number.)

If you are fitting the DAGUM model, scale the numbers to be less than 100, for example:

.001 5 10 15 25 35 50 75

but remember that your fitted results will be also scaled.

Next the screen should look like this:

```
ENTER NUM. OF CLASSES IF EQ 0 STOP 8
ENTER NAME OF COUNTRY AND YEAR OF SURVEY Male
Full-time Year-Round Workers 1999
```

ENTER CRITICAL VALUE OF CHI_SQUARE 1
ENTER INCOME CLASS ENDPOINTS FOR CLASSES 1 to 8
1 5000 10000 15000 25000 35000 50000 75000
ENTER THE NUM.OF PEOPLE IN EACH CLASS

We now enter the numbers in the Number column of the table. Leave a space between each one and press Enter after the last number.

698 1009 3217 9944 10712 12457 10914 8569

You will now have the following screen:

ENTER NUM. OF CLASSES IF EQ 0 STOP 8
ENTER NAME OF COUNTRY AND YEAR OF SURVEY Male
Full-time Year-Round Workers 1999
ENTER CRITICAL VALUE OF CHI_SQUARE 1
ENTER INCOME CLASS ENDPOINTS FOR CLASSES 1 to 8
1 5000 10000 15000 25000 35000 50000 75000
ENTER THE NUM.OF PEOPLE IN EACH CLASS
698 1009 3217 9944 10712 12457 10914 8569
INITIAL VALUES HAVE BEEN SET FOR THE PARAMETERS
IF YOU WOULD LIKE TO OVERIDE THESE ENTER 1

Next enter "0" unless you have your own estimates of the initial parameters.

The program will then search through about 20,000 sets of parameters for the model and select the set that has the lowest CHI-SQUARE. The table will be printed out with the best fit, including the parameters and the fitted values (FREQ CMPT). At this point you will be given the option to do another 20,000 iterations or to quit iterating. It is best to continue iterating until there are no more changes in the CHI SQUARE.

References

Adelman, Irma and Sherman Robinson, *Income Distribution Policies in Developing Countries: A Case Study of Korea*, Stanford, Stanford University Press, 1978.

Adelman, I., M. Hopkins, G. Rodgers, and R. Véry, *A Comparison of Two Models for Income Distribution Planning*, Journal of Policy Modelling, Vol. 1, 1979, pp. 37–82.

Ahluwalia, Montek S., *Inequality, Poverty and Development*, Journal of Development Economics, Vol. 3, 1976, pp. 307–342.

Ahluwalia, Montek S., Nicholas G. Carter, and Hollis B. Chenery, *Growth and Poverty in Developing Countries*, Journal of Development Economics Vol. 61979, pp. 1–79.

Aitchison, J. and J. A. Brown, *The Lognormal Distribution*, Cambridge, Cambridge University Press, 1957.

Atkinson, A. B., *On the Measurement of Inequality*, Journal of Economic Theory, Vol. 2, 1970, pp. 44–63.

———, *On the Measure of Poverty*, Econometrica, Vol. 55, No. 4, July 1987, pp. 749–764.

Barro, Robert J. and Xavier Sala-i-Martin, *Economic Growth*, second edition, Cambridge, Mass., MIT Press, 2004.

Bartels, C. P. A. and H. van Metelen, *Alternative Probability Density Functions of Income*, Research Memorandum No. 29, Amsterdam, Vrije University, 1975, pp. 1–30.

Berkson, J., *Maximum Likelihood and Minimum Chi-squared Estimates of the Logistic Function*, American Statistical Association Journal, March 1955, pp. 130–161.

Bhagwati, Jagdish, *In Defense of Globalization*, New York, Oxford University Press, 2004.

Bhalla, Surjit S., *Imagine There's No Country*, Washington, Institute for International Economics, 2002.

Birdsall, Nancy and Estelle James, *Efficiency and Equity in Social Spending: How and Why Governments Misbehave*, in Michael Lipton and Jacques van der Gang, eds., *Including the Poor*, Washington, World Bank, 1993.

Blackorby, Charles and David Donaldson, *Ethical Indices for the Measure of Poverty*, Econometrica, Vol. 48, No. 4, May 1980, pp. 1053–1060.

Blackwood, D. L. and R. G. Lynch, *The Measurement of Inequality and Poverty: A Policy Maker's Guide to the Literature, World Development*, Vol. 22, No. 4, 1994, pp. 567–578.

Campano, F., *A Fresh Look at Champernowne's Five-Parameter Formula*, Economie appliquée, Vol. 40, 1987, pp. 162–175.

Campano, Fred and Dominick Salvatore, *Economic Development, Income Inequality, and Kuznets' U-Shaped Hypothesis*, Journal of Policy Modeling, June 1988, pp. 265–280.

———, *Income Distribution in Africa*, in Dominick Salvatore, ed., *African Development Prospects/A Policy Modeling Approach*, New York, Taylor and Francis, 1989, p. 79.

———, *A Two-Sector Model, Two-Goods Model of Growth and Migration, and the Gini coefficient*, in Franz Haslinger and Oliver Stonner-Venlatarama, eds., *Aspects of Income Distribution*, Metropolis Verlag, 1998.

Champernowne, D. G., *The Graduation of Income Distributions*, Econometrica, No. 4, October 1952, pp. 591–615.

———, *A Comparison of Measures of Inequality of Income Distribution*, Economic Journal, No. 84, 1975, pp. 787–816.

Champernowne, D. G. and F. A. Cowall, *Economic Equality and Income Distribution*, Cambridge, Cambridge University Press, 1999.

Chen, Shaohua and Martin Ravallion, *How Have the World's Poor Fared since 1980?* World Bank Research Observer, Vol. 19, No. 2, 2004, pp. 141–169.

Civardi, Maisa B., *Income Multipliers in the Household Institutional Sector*, in C. Dagum and M. Zenga, eds., *Studies in Contemporary Economics: Income and Wealth Distribution, Inequality and Poverty*, Berlin, Springer-Verlag, 1990.

Cohen, Suleiman I., *Two Attempts to Extend Economic Models to Socio-Political Issues and Realities*, Pakistan Development Review, Vol. 19, No. 4, Winter 1980, pp. 282–310.

Congressional Budget Office, *Historical Effective Tax Rates, 1979–1997*, Washington, GPO, May 2001.

Cox, Michael W. and Richard Alm, *By our Own Bootstrings: Economic Opportunity and the Dynamics of Income Distribution*, Dallas, Tex., Federal Reserve Bank of Dallas, 1995.

Dagum, C., *A Model of Income Distribution and the Conditions of Existence of Moments of Finite Order*, Proceeding of the 40th session of the International Statistical Institute, Vol. 46, Book 3, Warsaw, 1975, pp. 196–202.

———, *A New Model of Personal Income Distribution: Specification and Estimtion*, Economie appliquée, Vol. 30, 1977, pp. 413–437.

———, *Linking the Functional and Personal Distributions of Income*, in Jacque Silber, ed., *Handbook of Income Inequality Measurement*, Kluwer Academic Press, 1999.

Danziger, Sheldon, Robert Haveman, and Eugene Smolensky, *The Measurement and Trend of Inequality: Comment*, American Economic Review, June 1977, pp. 505–512.

Deininger, Klaus and Lyn Squire, *New Ways of Looking at Old Issues: Inequality and Growth*, Journal of Development Economics, Vol. 57, 1998, pp. 259–287.

Dollar, David and Aron Kraay, *Growth Is Good for the Poor*, Policy Research Working Paper 2587, Washington, World Bank, 2001.

———, *Trade, Growth and Poverty*, Economic Journal, February, 2004, pp. 22–49.

Dunning, John H., ed., *Making Globalization Good*, New York, Oxford University Press, 2004.

Fields, Gary S., *Who Benefits from Economic Development? A Re-Examination of Brazilian Growth in the 1960s*, American Economic Review, September 1977, pp. 570–582.

———, *A Welfare Economic Approach to Growth and Distribution in the Dual Economy*, Quarterly Journal of Economics, August 1979, pp. 325–353.

———, *Changes in Poverty and Inequality in Developing Countries*, World Bank Research Observer, Vol. 4, No. 2, 1989, pp. 167–185.

Fisher, Gordon M., *The Development and History of the Poverty Thresholds*, Social Security Bulletin, Vol. 55, No. 4, 1992, pp. 1–24.

Fisk, P. R., *The Graduation of Income Distributions*, Econometrica, Vol. 29, 1961, pp. 171–185.

Forbes, Kristin, *A Reassessment of the Relationship Between Inequality and Growth*, American Economic Review, September 2000, pp. 869–887.

Formby, J. P. and Terry G. Seaks, *Paglin's Gini Measure of Inequality: A Modification*, American Economic Review, June 1980, pp. 479–482.

Formby, J. P., Terry G. Seaks, and W. James Smith, *On the Measurement and Trend of Inequality: A Reconsideration*, American Economic Review, March 1989, pp. 256–264.

Frankel, Jeffrey, *Globalization of the Economy*, NBER Working Paper 7858, August 2000.

Frosini, Benito V., *Comparing Inequality Measures*, Statistica, Vol. 45, No. 3, 1985, pp. 299–317.

Galbraith, James K., *Macroeconomics of Income Distributions*, in James K. Galbraith and Maureen Berner, eds., *Inequality and Change—A Global View*, Cambridge, Cambridge University Press, 2001.

———, *A Perfect Crime: Inequality in the Age of Globalization*, Daedalus, Winter 2002, pp. 11–25.

Gilbrat, R. *Les inégalités économique*, Paris, Siney, 1931.

Grilli, Enzo and Dominick Salvatore, *Economic Development*, Westport, Conn., Greenwood Press, 1994.

Harris, J. R. and M. P. Todaro, *Migration, Unemployment and Development: A Two-sector Analysis*, American Economic Review, Vol. 60, No. 1, 1970, pp. 126–142.

Hopkins, M. and R.Van der Hoven, *Economic and Social Factors in Development: A Socio-economic Framework for Basic Needs Planning*, WEP 2–32/WP 32, Geneva, ILO, November 1981.

Intal, P. S. and M. C. S. Bantilan, *Understanding Poverty and Inequality in the Philippines*, Manila, National Economic and Development Authority and United Nations Development Programme, Manila, 1994.

International Monetary Fund, *The IMF's Poverty Reduction and Growth Facility (PRGF)*, Factsheet, September 2002.

———, *World Economic Outlook*, Washington, IMF, April 2004.

Jain, S. *Size Distribution of Income: A Compilation of Data*, Washington, World Bank, 1975.

Johnson, William R., *The Measurement and Trend of Inequality: Comment*, American Economic Review, June 1977, pp. 502–504.

Kakwani, Nanak C., *Income Inequality and Poverty*, A World Bank Research Publication, New York, Oxford University Press, 1980.

Kloek, T. and H. K. Van Dijk, *Efficient Estimation of Income Distribution Parameters*, Journal of Econometrics 8, 1978, pp. 61–74.

Kravis, I. B., Z. Kenessey, A. Heston, and R. Summers, *A System of International Comparisons of Gross Product and Purchasing Power*, Baltimore, Md., Johns Hopkins University Press, 1975.

Kurien, C. John, *The Measurement and Trend of Inequality: Comment*, American Economic Review, June 1977, pp. 517–519.

Kuznets, S., *Economic Growth and Income Inequality*, American Economic Review, March 1955, pp. 1–28.

———, *Quantitative Aspects of the Economic Growth of Nations: Distribution of Income by Size*, Economic Development and Cultural Change, Vol. 11, No. 2, Pt. 2, Chicago, Chicago University Press 1963, pp. 1–79.

Lenti, Renata Targetti, *Income Distribution and the Structure of the Economic System: a SAM Approach*, in C. Dagum and M. Zenga eds., *Studies in Contemporary Economics: Income and Wealth Distribution, Inequality and Poverty*, Berlin, Springer-Verlag, 1990.

McKibbin, Warwick and Dominick Salvatore, *The Global Economic Consequences of the Uruguay Round*, Open Economies Review, April 1995, pp. 111–129.

Minarik, Joseph L., *The Measurement and Trend of Inequality: Comment*, American Economic Review, June 1977, pp. 513–516.

Nelson, Eric R., *The Measurement and Trend of Inequality: Comment*, American Economic Review, June 1977, pp. 497–501.

Paglin, Morton, *The Measurement and Trend of Inequality: A Basic Revision*, American Economic Review, September 1975, pp. 598–609.

———, *The Measurement and Trend of Inequality: Reply*, American Economic Review, June 1977, pp. 520–531.

Papanek, G. F. and O. Kyn, *The Effect on Income Distribution of Development, the Growth Rate and Economic Strategy*, Journal of Development Economics, Vol. 23, 1986, pp. 55–65.

Pareto, V., *Cours d'economique politique*, Rouge, Lausanne, 1897.

Pritchett, Lant, *Divergence, Big Time*, Journal of Economic Perspectives, No. 3, 1997, pp. 3–17.

Pyatt, Graham, *On the Interpretation and Disaggregation of Gini Coefficients*, Economic Journal, June 1976, pp. 243–55.

———, *A SAM Approach to Modelling*, Journal of Policy Modelling, No. 3, 1988, pp. 327–352.

Randolph, Susan M. and William F. Lott, *Can the Kuznets Effect be Relied on to Induce Equalizing Growth?*, World Development, Vol. 21, No. 5, 1993, pp. 829–840.

Ravallion, Martin and Benu Bidani, *How Robust is the Poverty Profile?*, World Bank Economic Review, Vol. 8, No. 1, 1994, pp. 75–102.

Ruggles, Patricia and Michael O'Higgins, *The Distribution of Public Expenditure among Households in the United States*, Review of Income and Wealth, Series 27, 1981, pp. 137–163.

Saith, Ashwani, *Development and Distribution—A Critique of the Cross-Country U-Hypothesis*, Journal of Development Economics, Vol. 13, 1983, pp. 367–382.

Sala-i-Martin, Xavier, *The World Distribution of Income*, NBER Working Paper 8933, May 2002.

Salem, A. B. Z. and T. D. Mount, *A Convient Descriptive Model of Income Distribution*, Econometrica, Vol. 42, 1974, pp. 1115–1127.

Salvatore, D., *Internal Migration, Urbanization, and Economic Development*, in D. Salvatore ed., *World Population Trends and Their Impact on Economic Development*, Westport, Conn., Greenwood Press, 1988.

———, *Protectionism and World Welfare*, New York, Cambridge University Press, 1993.

———, *International Trade and Economic Development*, Institutions and Economic Development, Fall 2003, pp. 5–26.

———, *Microeconomics: Theory and Applications*, fourth edition, New York, Oxford University Press, 2003.

Schwartz, Gerd and Teresa Ter-Minassian, *The Distributional Effects of Public Expenditure: Update and Overview*, IMF Working Paper wp/95/84, Washington, International Monetary Fund, 1995.

Sen, A. K., *Poverty: An Ordinal Approach to Measurement*, Econometrica, Vol. 44, March, 1976, pp. 219–231.

Singh, S. K. and G. S. Maddala, *A Function for the Size Distribution of Incomes*, Econometrica, Vol. 44, 1976, pp. 481–486.

Stern, Nicholas, *A Strategy for Development*, Washington, World Bank, 2002.

Stiglitz, Joseph, *Globalization and Its Discontents*, New York, 2002.

Suruga, T., *Functional Forms of Income Distribution: The Case of Yearly Income Groups in the "Annual Report on the Family Income and Expenditure Survey,"* Economic Studies Quarterly-The Journal of the Japan Association of Economics and Econometrics, April 1982, pp. 361–395.

Theil, Henri, *Economics and Information Theory*, North-Holland, Amsterdam, 1967.

Thurow, L. *Analysing the American Income Distribution*, American Economic Review, Vol. 48, 1970, pp. 261–269.

Tinbergen, J., *Income Distribution*, Amsterdam, North-Holland, 1975.

United Nations, *Enhancing Socio-Economic Policies in the Least Developed Countries of Asia*, New York, United Nations, 1999.

———, *Handbook of Input-Output Table Compilation and Analysis*, New York, United Nations, 1999.

United Nations Development Programme, *Human Development Report 2002*, New York, Oxford University Press, 2002.

———, *Human Development Report 2003*, New York, Oxford University Press, 2003.

United States Catholic Conference, *Economic Justice for All, Catholic Social Teaching and the U.S. Economy*, Third Draft, Publication No. 998, Washington, June, 1986.

U.S. Census Bureau, *Money Income in the United States, 1998*, P60–206, Washington, GPO, 1999.

———, *Money Income in the United States 1999*, P60–209, Washington, GPO, 2000.

Wertz, Kenneth L., *The Measurement and Trend of Inequality: Comment*, American Economic Review, September, 1979, pp. 670–671.

Wong, John and Sritua Arief, *An Overview of Income Distribution in South Korea, Hong Kong, Indonesia, Malaysia, The Philippines, Singapore and Thailand*, South East Asian Economic Review, Vol. 5, No. 1, 1984, pp. 1–66.

The World Bank, *Social Indicators of Development 1995*, Baltimore, Md., Johns Hopkins University Press, 1995.

———, *World Development Report 2000/2001*, NewYork, Oxford University Press, 2001.

———, *World Development Indicators*, Washington DC, World Bank, 2002.

———, *Globalization, Growth and Poverty: Building an Inclusive World Economy*, New York, Oxford University Press, 2003.

World Commission on the Social Dimension of Globalization, *A Fair Globalization*, Geneva, ILO, 2004.

Name Index

Adelman, I., 150
Adelman, Irma, 150
Ahluwalia, Montek S., 110, 111, 113
Aitchison, J., 32
Alm, Richard, 131
Arief, Sritan, 111
Atkinson, A. B., 82, 91

Bantilan, M. C. S., 88
Barro, Robert J., 125
Bartels, C. P. A., 44
Berkson, J., 39
Bhagwati, Jagdish, 126
Bhalla, Surjit S., 123
Bidani, Benu, 88
Birdsall, Nancy, 133
Blackorby, Charles, 94
Blackwood, D. L., 91
Brown, J. A., 32

Campano, Fred, 57, 110–111, 136
Carter, Nicholas G., 111, 113
Champernowne, D. G., 44, 53, 80
Chenery, Hollis B. 111, 113
Civardi, Maisa B., 150
Cohen, Suleiman I., 144
Congressional Budget Office, 136
Cowall, F. A., 80
Cox, Michael W., 131

Dagum, C., 44, 51
Danziger, Sheldon, 78

Deininger, Klaus, 111
Dollar, David, 121
Donaldson, David, 94
Dunning, John H., 126

Fields, Gary S., 109, 111
Fisher, Gordon M., 88
Fisk, P. R., 44
Forbes, Kristin, 115
Formby, J. P., 79
Frankel, Jeffrey, 126
Frosini, Benito V., 80

Galbraith, James K., 106,
   112, 144
Gilbrat, R., 32, 44
Grilli, Enzo, 126

Harris, J. R., 109
Haveman, Robert, 78
Heston, A., 104
Hopkins, M., 144

IMF (2004), World Economic
   Outlook, 126
Intal, P. S., 12, 88
International Monetary
   Fund, 98

Jain, S., 110–111
James, Estelle, 133
Johnson, William R., 78

Kakwani, Nanak C., 32, 67, 88
Kenessey, Z., 104
Kloek, T., 39, 45
Kraay, Aron, 121
Kravis, I. B., 104
Kurien, C. John, 79
Kuznets, Simon, 24, 107

Lenti, Renata Targetti, 144
Lott, William F., 111
Lynch, R. G., 91

Maddala G. S., 44, 48
McKibbin, Warwick, 126
Minarik, Joseph L., 78
Mount, T.D., 44

Nelson, Eric R., 78

O'Higgins, Michael, 128

Paglin, Morton, 75
Papanek, G. F., 116
Pareto, V., 24, 44
Pritchett, Lant, 122
Pyatt, G., 78, 144

Randolph, Susan M., 111
Ravallion, Martin, 88, 124
Robinson, Sherman, 150
Rodgers, G., 150
Ruggles, Patricia, 128

Saith, Ashwani, 111
Sala-i-Martin, Xavier, 123

Salem, A. B. Z, 44
Salvatore, D., 13, 109–111, 126
Schwartz, Gerd, 133
Seaks, Terry G., 79
Sen, A. K., 92
Singh, S. K., 44, 48
Smith, W. James, 79
Smolensky, Eugene, 78
Squire, Lyn, 111
Stern, Nicholas, 126
Stiglitz, Joseph, 122
Summers, R., 104
Suruga, T., 45

Ter-Minassian, Teresa, 133
Theil, Henri, 81
Thurow, L., 44
Tinbergen, J., 9
Todaro, M. P., 109

U.S. Census Bureau, 13, 23, 28
United Nations, 104, 122, 136, 151
United Nations Development
    Programme, 101

Van der Hoven, R., 144
Van Dijk, H. K., 39, 45
van Metelen, H., 44
Véry, R., 150

Wertz, Kenneth L., 79
Wong, John, 112
World Bank, 11, 12, 104, 126
World Commission on the Social
    Dimension of Globalization, 126

Subject Index

Africa, 97, 124
Asia, 97, 112, 120–121, 124

basic needs, 4, 7, 11, 127

Canada, 45, 100–101, 114–117
consumer, 4, 17, 145
cummulative distribution function,
  27–28, 47, 50, 53–54, 89
current population reports, 16

decile, 7, 9, 58–67, 87, 110, 113, 130,
  133–135, 160
density function, 7, 24–32
developed countries, 5, 14–18, 24,
  87, 95–97, 105–108, 111, 114, 127,
  130, 132
developing countries, 5, 14–18, 72,
  87, 91, 95–97, 105–108, 110–112,
  114, 132–133, 144
direct search, 36–37
distribution of income, 3, 7

earnings, 26, 73
education, 4, 6, 17, 26
elasticity, 51
exchange rate, 22, 98–101

Gini coefficient, 58, 63–67, 72–80, 82,
  89–90, 92, 100–101
globalization, 117–124

goodness of fit, 33–43
government, 117–124
grouped data, 28, 36, 46
growth, 10–14, 51, 90, 95–96,
  98, 101, 105–114, 117–124

household, 1–2, 4–5, 7, 10–13, 17,
  20–21, 24–25, 33, 72–78,
  86–87, 99, 102–103, 110,
  127–131, 138–139, 141–143, 148
Human Development Index (HDI),
  101–102
human wants, 4–5

income, 14–18
income density models, 27, 44–57
India, 11
inequality, 59, 64, 71–82, 89–92, 106–
  112, 138
inflation, 9, 74, 95
input-output models, 137–148

Kuznets, 24, 106–112, 137–138, 143

labor, 4–5, 9, 71, 74, 88, 109, 140
Latin America, 97
lognormal distribution, 27–31,
  33–39, 44–46, 48, 55, 59–61
long-term models, 137–143
Lorenz curve, 58, 63–67, 72,
  75–80

marginal tax rate, 3–4, 128–131
mean, 6, 11, 28–31, 33–34, 49, 54,
    56, 58–61, 76–77, 80–82, 88–92,
    129–130

Pareto, 24, 44, 54, 92
per capita income, 4, 6, 11–12, 89,
    95–103, 105, 110–115, 134–135,
    138–140, 120–124
Philippines, 11, 25, 51, 88, 93–97,
    99, 112
poverty, 3–4, 7, 11–12, 51,
    86–93, 97–98, 110–112, 130,
    133–135
production, 4–5, 9, 107–108,
    117–119, 145
public expenditure, 127–133
purchasing power parity (PPP),
    22, 98–101

quantiles, 9, 26, 33, 58–62, 65,
    102–103, 153–157
quintiles. *See* quantiles

redistribution of income, 10,
    160, 127–135

savings, 10, 18, 107
short-term models, 143–150
social accounting matrices (SAM),
    146–150
standard of living, 5, 87, 96–103, 120
summary measures, 58–71
summary tables, 19–21
surveys, 7, 15, 17–18, 22, 33, 45–46,
    48, 72–73, 105, 110

taxation, 128
transfer of income, 108–110
two-sector models, 108–110

United States, 6, 10–11, 14, 16, 19–20,
    24, 29, 31, 56, 72–76, 86–87, 90,
    93, 96–98, 100–102, 105, 115–119,
    122–123, 127–128, 130–131,
    138–139, 141–143
U-shaped hypothesis. *See* Kuznets